FREE TRADE OR PROTECTION?

A Pragmatic Analysis

H. Peter Gray

*Professor of Economics and Finance
Rutgers University*

St. Martin's Press   New York

All rights reserved. For information, write:
St. Martin's Press, Inc., 175 Fifth Avenue, New York, NY 10010
Printed in Hong Kong
Published in the United Kingdom by The Macmillan Press Ltd.
First published in the United States of America in 1985

ISBN 0-312-30374-2

Library of Congress Cataloging in Publication Data
Gray, H. Peter.
    Free trade or protection?
    Bibliography: p.
    Includes index.
    1. Free trade and protection. I. Title.
HF1713.G585 1985   382.7   85-11930
ISBN 0-312-30374-2

*To those economists who recognise the need for
and do not shun the difficulty of analyses of
reactions to evolution, institutional change and
substantial changes in underlying conditions*

Contents

Preface

For many years I have had the growing impression that the discipline of economics has sought to solve problems which were capable of solution in an elegant way: the art-form lay in restricting the number of assumptions needed for a mathematically-precise solution. This set of problems is to be contrasted with those which provide untidy solutions at best but do reflect the complexities of the world around us. Very little attention is paid in economics to consideration of the different types of disturbances or shocks which can impinge on an economy and of how the appropriate policy response (including passivity) might vary according to the kind of disturbance. Some of this failure to concern itself with different types of disturbances can be traced to the infatuation of the discipline with cyclical problems following the Great Depression and with the refinement of Keynes's *General Theory*. The success of so-called Keynesian policies in the 20 years after the Second World War could have produced a tranquil state of mind among economists: in the language of this book, problems of resource reallocation which arose were 'benign' because the changes came so slowly that they were well within the capacity of the system to adjust without serious dislocation.

If one ignores disturbances, one works in a domain of steady-state equilibrium and this is the arena in which the debate of free trade or protection has traditionally been conducted. In such an arena, free trade always wins. But the reality of our world is one in which disturbances come in different shapes and sizes and at different frequencies. A tranquil world of minor disturbances can quickly change to a state of turbulence in which major reallocations of resources are forced on national economies: recent events have shifted a world of virtual tranquillity or suppressed changes to one in which changes must be accommodated. This is a very different arena and in this arena the relative merits of free trade or protection take on new perspectives: indeed, the perspective changes according to the kind of disturbance with which the system is afflicted.

At the risk of taking liberties with the concepts of Jan Tinbergen

(1970), it is possible to present the issues considered in this book as a consideration of the policies which can best accommodate qualitative change. Tinbergen distinguishes between quantitative and qualitative policies: qualitative policies involve the changing of some aspect of economic structure, while quantitative policies involve changes in certain parameters within the same economic structure. Tinbergen's analysis seems to limit his consideration of qualitative policies to those required to bring about a change which follows from the emergence of a new general interest function for the economy (1970, pp. 68–73). This book is concerned with a more difficult problem: what policies should be used to best adapt an economy with an unchanging general interest function to a new set of economic conditions in world markets? To quote Tinbergen: 'the scientific treatment of qualitative policy meets with great difficulties' (1970, p. 72).

My interest in commercial policy and in the process of adjustment began many years ago with a thought about the possibility of the need for phase-out protection. (I learned while writing this book that Ricardo had broached the same issue about 150 years earlier!) Phase-out protection only becomes a matter of concern when some factors are industry- or product-specific. This was an outgrowth of a concern with the limitations of a body of trade theory based on generic factors of production. From this standpoint came my concern with the creation of a theory of international trade which would be broad enough to allow for the existence of industry-specific factors, intra-industry trade and multinational corporations. Any theory of international trade which does not encompass the existence of multinational corporations is misleading and the dynamic features of multinationals require that international trade theory not be confined to a domain of steady-state, long-run general equilibrium.

The other seed from which this book sprang is Canterbery's vita theory of income distribution which addresses itself to the problems of skill-levels and skill acquisition. The vita theory proved to be the Rosetta Stone which enabled me to formulate all my misgivings about the interaction of rapid changes in trade patterns and the rate of employment in industrialised nations. I am greatly indebted to E. Ray Canterbery for his endless patience in explaining the subtleties of his theory. I am also particularly indebted to Ingo Walter with whom I have had ongoing discussions about international trade and commercial policy spread over many years. Detlef Lorenz and Thomas A. Pugel have both contributed to my understanding of this arcane area of economics.

I wish to acknowledge the courtesy of the Eastern Economic Association and the Indian Institute of Foreign Trade in New Delhi for allowing me to reproduce material first published in the *Eastern Economic Journal* and the *Foreign Trade Review*. I am obliged to the Trade Policy Research Centre for permission to quote extensively from one of its *International Issues* series entitled 'MFA Forever?'

This book seeks to reconsider the possibility that protective measures might be useful features of international economic policy in a turbulent world. Nothing in the book suggests that, within the confines of their assumptions, the models of advocates of free trade are incorrect: the argument is merely that reality and the assumptions of free traders part company when the world is undergoing rapid evolution. Some proponents of free trade cleave to their doctrine with what amounts to a religious fervour. I hope that they will do my book the courtesy of considering the arguments dispassionately. If they disagree with the arguments put forward here, I would ask only that they set down exactly what assumptions they have to make (or refuse to grant me) in order to render my arguments invalid. The most probable candidate is the assertion that, once protection is instituted on behalf of an industry, that protection is locked in for eternity: if such be the case then free trade may be the best rule of economic policy formulation even in turbulent times, but it will be a poor reflection on the stuff of which economists and politicians are made.

Belle Mead, New Jersey, USA   H. PETER GRAY

1 The Present Need to Reconsider the Free-Trade Doctrine

Forty years after the end of the Second World War, the momentum for greater freedom of international trade has been exhausted. The Tokyo Round was its last hurrah. These forty years of remarkable gains in the reduction of impediments to international trade, and in the volume of international trade, may come to be known as the golden years of the General Agreement of Tariffs and Trade (the GATT). Now, in the eighties, the forces of protectionism are gaining strength and clamour against imports is heard throughout the industrial world. Ranged against these resurgent forces for protectionism are conservative politicians who have complete faith in the workings of a system of markets, and a hard core of international economists who rank any departure from unsullied free trade with one of the deadly sins. Both groups cleave to the doctrine of free trade with something approaching a religious fervour. This fervour, on the part of the economists at least, probably derives from the destructiveness of the protectionism of the thirties, and possibly from the preoccupation of modern economics with formal welfare analyses. There is a close affinity between the orthodox, factor-proportions theory of international trade, and the derivative doctrine of free trade, and welfare economics. Both are based on models which are severely constrained in their applicability to reality by the assumptions under which they are developed. Both are set in general equilibrium with its deemphasis of both abstract and historical time. Both concern themselves entirely with allocative efficiency so that no consideration is given to income–distributional aspects, which are designated as normative. Consumers are assumed to be rational price-takers so that the relative prices which they face must represent relative opportunity costs of production. Given the large number of assumptions which limit the applicability of the pure, orthodox theory of international

1

trade to reality (and the assumptions listed above are only a small sample of the population), the fervour of the commitment to the doctrine of free trade is surprising.

The purpose of this book is to consider possible qualifications to an uncompromising stance in favour of free trade that derive from the release of assumptions used in the underlying model. Any policy recommendation that derives from a theoretical construct is valid and relevant only if the assumptions which underlie the theory are compatible with the world in which the policies are being instigated. It will be argued that some of the assumptions on which the free-trade doctrine is indirectly based are not appropriate to the world of the eighties and beyond. In consequence the pure free-trade doctrine may need to be tempered with a dash of realism. The so-called pragmatic aspect of the study relies on the choice of assumptions called into question. These assumptions will be those considered by the author to have serious implications for policy at the present time. There is an inevitable degree of subjectivity involved. The alternative is to adopt a taxonomic approach which would examine the implications of relinquishing each assumption in turn (as well as appropriate combinations of assumptions) for the validity of an uncompromising free-trade doctrine.

It is *not* the purpose of this book to argue that protection is, in some absolute sense, more beneficial than free trade. It is *not* the purpose of this book to argue against some general proposition that, under the conditions implicitly assumed by advocates of free trade, more trade is better than less trade. It is the purpose of this book to consider the argument that the conditions implicit in the free-trade doctrine may not be those which prevail at some stages of economic history, and that at such times, *an unquestioning commitment to free trade can lead economists to shun important problems.* John Maynard Keynes (1936, ch. 23) considered a time of recovery from the depth of a depression to be a time when renunciation of free trade might be warranted. He would probably not have made that assertion had he been able to rely upon all industrial nations adopting similar, harmonized policies so that rates of economic expansion would have been roughly equal (Gray, 1979, pp. 590–1). In a world in which real shocks and disturbances are large and/or follow hard upon one another, a total commitment to free trade may need to be questioned.

Two assumptions of the orthodox theory of international trade will form the basis for most of the qualifications of the free-trade doctrine to be developed here. These are the assumptions of a static or timeless general equilibrium solution, and of the compatibility of the free-trade equilibrium with a satisfactory level of employment in industrialised countries. The emphasis, then, is on the costs of adjustment of economies to changes in global conditions. These changes can take place within economies or among economies, and will constitute disturbances or shocks. Economies must reallocate resources in line with the new conditions if the free-trade doctrine is followed. The reallocation may be excessively costly if carried out at some 'natural' or 'laisser-passer' rate, or the new conditions may require the sacrifice of some economic goal. If some economic goal is to be sacrificed, free trade may be the goal that is the least costly to sacrifice.

In an extremely disappointing paper, Deardorff and Stern (1983) purport to address the limitations, if any, of the free-trade argument if the assumptions underlying its theoretical basis are not valid: 'The question that naturally arises is whether the model of free trade is appropriate and useful when one or more of its assumptions do not hold'. The authors identify as one of the assumptions of the free-trade model that there is 'ample time for markets to adjust'. Despite this, Deardorff and Stern proceed to neglect any limitations to the free-trade argument imposed by the static quality of the underlying theory, and review a series of qualifications within a framework of (timeless) general equilibrium. The one reference in the paper which might be expected to bear upon the problems of adjustment considers the existence of a domestic distortion, such as 'a difficulty of adjustment in the labor market. But if such a distortion exists, it would be better dealt with directly by domestic policy in its own right rather than by a countervailing duty'. There is something of a *deus ex machina* here, since the authors assume the tractability of the domestic distortion with the same ease they assume its existence.

The emphasis of this book is, then, on the various dimensions of the adjustment of economies to changes in global conditions. What is important here is the nature of the changes in the global conditions, their frequency, the irreversibility and whether or not the shocks are self-reinforcing or self-cancelling. One of the areas of weakness of formal economics is its failure to consider, in some positive manner, variation in the kind, size and frequency of disturbances. One should not, however, labour under the belief that all shocks are bad since they involve adjustment costs. Growth-generating forces are shocks to which adjustment must be made, and these disturbances are part and parcel of the 'churning effect' by which old industries die and new, more vital industries evolve. Old industries are relocated in developing countries as comparative advantage changes over time. Any adjustment requires reallocation of factors of production, and entails social costs. The question to be faced is how can the benefit/cost ratio be maximised. Nothing, then, precludes straightforward advocacy of free trade.

It is useful to conceive of adjustment costs as having three different degrees of severity: benign, accelerated and chronic. *Benign* adjustment takes place when an industry is forced to reduce output at a rate below that at which industry-specific human capital is considered to depreciate as the workers, in whom it is embodied, leave the work force voluntarily. Younger workers will gain employment in the expanding sectors of the economy, and the social costs of adjustment are negligible. *Accelerated* adjustment occurs when an industry is being forced to contract at a rate which involves displacing workers and closing down erstwhile productive capacity so quickly that industry-specific human and physical capital become valueless. *Chronic* adjustment costs are experienced when a country cannot reemploy factors of production displaced by the new conditions. This is the essence of structural unemployment when the skills and skill-levels required by job vacancies do not match the skills of the unemployed, or the skill levels to which they may aspire. This is a clear example of market failure. Some economists would consider chronic adjustment as a very long drawn out version of accelerated adjustment on the presumption that the comfortable neoclassical equilibrium will ultimately prevail in the labour market. According to Deardorff and Stern (1983) this would involve a domestic distortion, which would be cured either by market forces or with the help of some 'domestic policy'. Within the neoclassical framework, displaced workers will upgrade their skill levels to those demanded by industry, and industry will adjust its needs for workers of different skills. Both forces will be responses to an increase in the differences in the wage rates of skilled and unskilled workers. Such a process will take longer than Marshall's long run, as it is usually understood, and can be considered to require at least the very long run.[1] The distinction between chronic and accelerated adjustment will be maintained in this book, and is developed in greater detail below. However, it is acknowledged that a condition of excess skill-deficient labour could be eradicated in the very long run, but it is also asserted that there can be no assurance that any such excess will in fact be eradicated without active and continuing policy intervention. The neoclassical solution cannot be disproven, but neither can it be proven to hold.[2] If the implicit condition of neoclassical analysis – that the wage rate shall allow workers and their families a subsistence income – is specified, the probability that the neoclassical solution will be attained is substantially reduced.

The possibility of what amounts to permanent involuntary unemployment will require a major rethinking of social programmes and social values. International competition is only one contributing force to the problem, but it is likely to prove an important one. It is useful here to anticipate briefly the arguments of Chapters 5, 6 and 7, and to sketch in the outline of the problem which may provide the biggest economic challenge for economic policy makers in industrial countries since the depression of the thirties. Social programmes must countenance a system providing adequate financial support for what could be a lifetime of unemployment. In the US, and possibly in other countries, the whole apparatus of economic support systems will need to be overhauled. In the US, unemployment compensation lasts for six months, although in deep recessions it can be extended to nine months. After the expiration of these benefits, the worker and family become dependent upon the less generous (and socially-stigmatizing) system of 'welfare.' Old-age retirement benefits are determined by deductions from wages and salaries during a lifetime of employment, and vary with the length of employment and the salaries received. In the face of large-scale, permanent unemployment, old people would also be consigned to the welfare rolls. Failure to revise the economic support systems would be likely to generate severe social costs. But there is another dimension. In a society in which the Puritan ethic plays an important role, there is a stigma to unemployment which can have serious consequences for individuals. Either one develops an immunity to the system by developing a 'welfare mentality', in which event one's employability is seriously reduced, or guilt may prey upon the mind. In a study of the sensitivity of social variables to the level of unemployment, Brenner (1976) showed clearly that society functioned less well when unemployment rates were high: suicides increased as did commitments to state mental institutions, death by cirrhosis of the liver and murders. It is possible that people will maintain their employability while developing an insouciance towards unemployment, but this will not happen quickly. A society likely to be afflicted with widespread and very long run unemployment may need to revise both its economic systems and its sets of values. In such a process, free trade cannot be considered sacrosanct.

Hager (1982) takes a different approach. Focusing directly upon the effect on the social fabric of the industrialised European nations of rapid increases in imports or manufactures from the Third World, he posits that achieved solutions to age-old problems of class warfare and income distribution will be destroyed. The integration of North/South markets will break the income and security bargains developed between the middle class and wage earners. Europe could change from a stabilising centre of calm in a politically turbulent world.

If the conditions prevailing in the real world do not conform to those implied by the assumptions of the theory of international trade on which the free-trade doctrine rests, there may be wisdom in considering a different set of policies. This is not to argue that the analyst will renounce the goals of adherence to the free-trade doctrine which are to maximise efficiency. It does suggest that the common set of goals may allow a better final package of policies to be attained than will be generated by an unswerving advocacy of uncompromising free trade. A model which identifies the costs of adjustment may permit the creation of a package which places emphasis on continued pressure to adjust on threatened industries. This may achieve a better economic system in the long run than would follow from advocacy of a laisser-passer world with all the potential of such a world for political lobbying and obdurate protectionism. Hager (1982) suggests that a failure to recognize the danger that a flood of manufactured imports into Europe will result in a rash of piecemeal and sudden protectionist policies applied haphazardly across industries according to their political 'clout'. This he terms 'panic protectionism', and suggests that it will give the worst of all outcomes to the countries involved. One need only consider the rash of industrial policies in Europe (carefully reported in Curzon Price, 1981) to see the danger that Hager's forebodings may prove correct.

Chapter 2 summarises the theory underlying the doctrine of free trade. Chapter 3 introduces Harvey Leibenstein's concept of X-efficiency into the theory of international trade. This new dimension adds to the strength of the arguments for free trade and, at the same time, presents an argument for a particular kind of protection when industries are temporarily X-inefficient. Chapter 4 looks at the problem of the rate of adjustment. This argument relies directly upon Canterbery's vita theory (1979), which is presented in more formal detail in Appendix A. Chapter 5 considers the possibility that the industrialised nations are doomed to be faced with permanent involuntary unemployment. The analysis in this chapter also rests heavily on Canterbery's theory because the vita theory emphasises the mechanism by which workers can and will upgrade their skills. Chapter 6 is concerned with the international dimensions of the permanent unemployment of low-skilled workers. Chapter 7 offers some suggestions for policy and for policy implementation. The suggestions are necessarily tentative because of the difficulties in promoting upgrading of workers, and because of the limits to the abilities of governments to intervene to correct the kind of problems which are being faced. An ideal solution is not feasible. Just as fine tuning has proven to be a theoretical extravagance in macroeconomics, so too are the so-called optimal intention policies in international trade (Blackhurst, 1981). Chapter 8 is concerned with problems impeding a free-trade area among the industrialised world.

The obverse of free trade is 'protection' which can be defined as any policy measure which discriminates between home and foreign suppliers, or between import substitutes and non-tradeable goods. In practice, protection covers a wide range of policies, from the simple and straightforward *ad valorem* tariff to such arcane non-tariff barriers as packaging and health requirements. This book does not distinguish between the different ways of protecting domestic producers from foreign competition: it will assume, with an appreciable amount of heroism, that a bureaucracy will always use the device that most efficiently achieves its purpose.[3] Some reference will be made to this issue in Chapter 7, but its gist will be to reinforce the neoclassical tenet that a subsidy to the home producer is usually, if not always, the least costly measure from the point of view of global efficiency.

2 The Argument for Free Trade and its Underlying Assumptions

Adam Smith and David Ricardo both played important roles in the development of the theory of international trade. Both argued strongly for free trade on the basis that gains from trade were universally available. Both economists were concerned with reducing the degree of protection from very high levels, and both were writing in that period of surging dynamism, the industrial revolution. Smith was primarily concerned with the elimination of involvement on the part of government in economic matters: his doctrine of the efficiency of the invisible hand relied upon the existence of effective competition among firms. Smith's advocacy of free trade relied on the existence of gains from trade *and* a more competitive economy. Ricardo was a major intellectual force behind the repeal of the Corn Laws in the UK in 1846. Neither argument was laid out with an explicit set of assumptions, but Smith (1976, Book IV, ch. 2) did countenance the need for some gradualism in the rate of reduction of protective measures. He found even this argument exaggerated on the grounds that workers 'thrown out of one employment would easily find another'. The classical assumption of full employment and the spontaneity of its attainment was a basic component of the argument. Mill's refutation of protection is standard. The argument is presented in a chapter entitled, 'Of Interferences of Government Grounded on Erroneous Theories,' and the text leads into the subject matter with, 'Of these false theories, the most notable is the doctrine of Protection to Native Industry' (Mill, 1909, p. 917).

All three classical authors were prepared to make exception in terms of the national defence, but in little else. The arguments were, in modern terms, long-run, static equilibrium approaches in which full employment was a natural state. The arguments did not encompass the idea of labour having any significant heterogeneity. The reliance

8

on perfect competition within the domestic industry was so strong that Mill even went so far as to divorce protection from any increase in profit in the domestic (protected) industry, except in basic agriculture (Mill, 1909, p. 917). In an era and country in which rapid growth was taking place spontaneously, and in which huge corporations had not yet evolved, these assumptions may have been less heroic than they may appear in the latter years of the twentieth century.

Ricardo did address the costs of change in chapter 19 of his *Principles* (Ricardo, 1911). In a chapter entitled 'On Sudden Changes in the Channels of Trade' Ricardo observes the frictional costs of adjustment to new sets of trading conditions. In the process, he sketches in the idea of phase-out or senile-industry protection (p.178). The analysis is disappointing. Labour is considered homogeneous:

> It is often impossible to divert the machinery which may have been erected for one manufacture to the purposes of another; but the clothing, the food, and the lodging of the labourer in one employment maybe devoted to the support of the labourer in another; or the same labourer may receive the same food, clothing and lodging, whilst his employment is changed. (p. 177)

But the focus of the chapter is more political tract than analysis and the subject matter soon shifts to agriculture and the transition from war to peace and the implications of such a change for the rent earned on land. The world is one in which transitory costs of adjustment are to be tolerated in exchange for the perpetuity of gains from free trade in static equilibrium.

The existence of gains from trade is the basis for the modern formal argument for free trade. Samuelson (1939) proves the existence of gains from trade in a competitive equilibrium. If the effects of international trade on individuals were dismissed – either by assuming that individuals are identical in tastes or by assuming that gainers could compensate losers – the existence of gains from trade establishes the argument for free trade. Free trade will generate the greatest level of output for a given global resource endowment, and any measure which restricts the free flow of goods and services among nations must necessarily reduce global output, and if any effects on individuals are neglected, global welfare. The proof is still less precise than later work in welfare economics so that the assumptions underlying the model are neither as clearly laid out nor as constraining. Samuelson proves that no matter what the global set of commodity and factor prices may be, there is always gain from trade to be had. Since the argument is couched uniquely in terms of a country adapting from an autarchic position to one of involvement in international trade as price-taker, the model falls short of a positive proof of a free-trade optimum although it undoubtedly set the stage for work which was to follow. Its assumptions are imposing: all the trappings of welfare analysis in the form of perfect markets, homogeneous factors, each product is produced with general factors, static full employment but factor supplies are variable.

The *locus classicus* of the formal presentation of the argument for free trade is Meade's *Trade and Welfare* (1955, ch. IX). This classic work is presented in taxonomic prose, which in its leisurely pace is reminiscent of Marshall's *Principles*. In taxonomic prose, assumptions are introduced gradually and a reader is forced to search for them. Sheer efficiency in communication would argue for the assumptions to be presented starkly. What follows is a distillation of Meade's case with the assumptions clearly identified.

Meade's case for free trade is in terms of formal welfare economics with the criterion for optimality defined as the maximisation of the sum of individual economic welfares. Equity considerations are allowed to intrude under certain conditions, but the subjective element of such judgments is emphasised. As is traditional with welfare economics, the analysis is static and general equilibrium. Moreover, the analysis is limited to marginal adjustments, in contrast with major structural shifts whose *mutatis mutandis* effects could not be estimated with reasonable accuracy. This restriction is important since it implies that any change in resource reallocation will be small. There is, therefore, no need for the analyst to study the costs of moving from one equilibrium position to another. Problems of adjustment may be neglected. Rather than hide this fact, Meade (1955, p. 52) assumes explicitly 'that there are no real costs of movements of factors when they turn from one industry to another'. It is not clear whether this assumption applies to costs of dislocation, including unemployment, or simply to costs of movement and retraining. Nations are assumed to be fully employed with balanced payments. If capital flows take place, the capital exporter is to reduce its money income to permit an offsetting surplus on the current account (Meade, 1955, p. 473).

Welfare is maximised when four conditions are met: (a) The exchange of a given volume of output is optimised so that no different distribution can improve the economic welfare of one person without damaging the welfare of another. This is optimisation of trade and applies domestically and internationally; (b) Production is maximised so that it is not possible to produce more of one good without producing less of another by a redistribution of inputs; (c) Production is optimised when the mix of goods demanded by consumers and the mix of production are mutually consistent; (d) Effort is optimised when each individual correctly values leisure in terms of additional income forgone. This condition implies the full-employment assumption (made above). In practice, this condition is subsumed within national economies and will not be referred to again in the context of international trade.

Each nation adopts a policy of what Meade calls 'modified laissez-faire' which allows people to consume and work as price-takers with perfect freedom. Government's economic measures are limited to those which are required to remove divergences between marginal social values and costs (Meade, 1955, p. 51). This policy implies that all money costs and prices of goods represent relative opportunity costs of production, therefore perfect competition exists in product markets. Similarly, all factors of production are paid their marginal product (opportunity costs) and perfect competition prevails in the factor markets. Because factors of production can be employed in many industries, the homogeneity of factors of production is assumed. This homogeneity is also implicit in the discussion of the optimum population (Meade, 1955, pp. 82-93). An inquiry into optimum population and optimum rates of saving does allow a measure of dynamism to creep into the analysis, which is otherwise constrained by the usual assumptions of fixed factor availabilities and given technology. Since the question of the population size is not mentioned in the discussion of free trade, there must be as well an implicit assumption that workers in all countries have marginal products in excess of what Meade calls 'the welfare subsistence level'. The question of workers being able to earn the welfare subsistence level has important real-world implications for the rest of this century (see Chapter 5 below). Similarly, the failure of workers in one country to earn the welfare subsistence level could be used to validate free movement of factors of production (see the discussion of Krauss's arguments below in this chapter) or even to justify international transfers from rich to poor countries. Both these problems are outside Meade's analytic domain since they must be seen as involving structural change or disequilibria. The measures which generate modified laissez-faire policy are called, appropriately, utopian domestic economic policies. Free trade is then shown to be the international complement to these policies for the maximisation of global economic welfare.

The case for free trade is then presented in a two-good, two-country framework, with homogeneous factors of production which are internally mobile and internationally immobile. To establish the case for free trade in line with the assumptions of modified laissez-faire in each country, 'it is easy to show that the marginal conditions for world economic efficiency require the free movement of products between world markets, which are so arranged that there are no divergencies between marginal social values and costs in any international transactions' (Meade, 1955, p. 149). The 'proof' relies on the familiar set of conditions for optimising trade and production and maximising production. The 'proof' is much more general than manipulations within the Heckscher–Ohlin–Samuelson model, for example, in that it deals purely with numerical examples (a more mathematical version is available in Meade, 1956). In this format, there is no need to specify precisely the assumptions made about tastes or factor supplies.

Optimisation of trade requires that the ratio of the prices of the two goods be equal in both countries. Maximisation of production requires that the ratio of marginal costs be equal, and the optimisation of production requires that the ratio of prices to marginal costs be equal in both countries. These conditions can only exist in the absence of man-made impediments to international trade (other than those required to achieve what Meade describes as 'modified free trade'). Much of the rhetoric of Third World nations addresses this possibility. Modified free trade exists when governments interfere with the natural workings of international markets in order to eliminate any discrepancies between marginal social values and costs that may be inherent in those markets. In fact, Meade's argument and major contribution is the substantiation of policies of the 'second best'. In context, this argues for the use of government policies to counter any natural imperfections in the economic system. Meade's case is then a case for modified free trade, not for free trade in an absolute sense unless there are no imperfections in international markets.

The case for free trade as developed by Meade in the assumed absence of international transportation costs has the weakness that it effectively integrates into a single and efficient whole two disparate economies which are performing with full efficiency independently of each other. The process seems, somehow, too easy. It neglects questions of compatibility among nations, and this neglect was one of the primary sources of antipathy at Ohlin's Nobel Symposium between theorists working within the confines of the traditional theory of international trade and location-theorists, geographers and development economists who are concerned with the realities of the world (Ohlin *et al.*, 1977, pp. 96–8 and 550–6). The impediments to international trade that derive from differences in national characteristics are summarised under the concept of 'psychic distance' by students of the multinational corporation. In practice, psychic distance can be used to identify patterns of weakness in informational linkages (Törnqvist, 1977) as well as simple differences among nations in language, laws and culture. Like transportation costs, the introduction of these phenomena reduces the tidiness of the conclusions without altering the essentials of the argument. Meade demonstrates this with respect to transportation costs (1955, p. 147).

The argument for free trade is presented in an elegantly clear way in Meade's *A Geometry of the Theory of International Trade* (1952). The assumptions underlying this graphical presentation are those of normal welfare theory with the additional assumption that every individual has identical tastes (Meade, 1952, p. 1). Using production blocks to indicate production in a modified laissez-faire economy and community indifference curves to denote tastes, Meade derives trade indifference curves which show ordinal gains from trade deriving from specific combinations of goods traded for each country. These trade indifference curves, coupled with prospective terms of trade, can be used to generate the traditional Marshallian reciprocal-demand or offer curve. The more favourable the terms of trade, the greater the gains from trade and the higher the trade indifference curve reached. Therefore gains from trade increase as the 'trading point' or equilibrium moves along the offer curve and away from the origin. When any impediment to international trade is imposed by a trading partner, the foreign offer curve shifts inwards, and the trading point moves down the home offer curve toward the origin. If the home country retaliates, the trading point will now lie within the original area enclosed by the two free-trade offer curves and indicates a loss of gain from trade by both countries. If retaliation is incomplete, the possibility exists that *one* country can achieve a net gain. However, world welfare is reduced because the loss of the other country exceeds the benefit derived by the country which gains. This argument for a tariff (or protection) requires that the country have some ability to influence its (net barter) terms of trade through monopoly power (that is, a small country will be a price-taker in world markets and will not be able to use this device). The device is the so-called optimum tariff (but terms-of-trade tariff might have been a more felicitous name). Export subsidies by both nations will have similar results. A subsidy by one country, which completely offsets a tariff by its trading partner, will effect an income transfer from the former to the latter, but will achieve maximum welfare.

It is useful, at this juncture, to relate Meade's presentation (1955) of the case for free trade with the two assumptions, identified in Chapter 1 above, as being the basis for most of the qualifications of the free-trade doctrine with which the argument of this book is concerned. Problems of adjustment are not considered by Meade. The assumption that there exist no real costs of the transfer of factors between industries is an explicit negation of the adjustment problem. Even in the absence of such an assumption, a perpetuity of improved economic welfare (and perpetuity is implicit in timeless, general equilibrium) must ultimately outweigh any transitory costs of adjustment unless the complexities of intergenerational transfers are countenanced. The difference between temporary and permanent changes in underlying economic conditions is not considered because of the focus of the analysis on whether the allocation of a given resource base and the consequent static conditions can be improved. This omission is somewhat surprising given that *Trade and Welfare* is the second volume in a series on international economic policy, and the final chapter of *Trade and Welfare* draws conclusions which cover the analyses of both the balance-of-payments volume and the welfare volume. Temporary distortions in the flows of payments are quite common, and balance-of-payments theory recognises such conditions as a reason for maintaining international reserves to avoid temporary dislocations being enforced on industries. Finally, the tacit assumption that workers earn the 'welfare subsistence level' (in the argument for modified free trade), and the explicit recognition that a set of analyses based on marginal changes cannot realistically be used to analyse structural change, exclude consideration of the possibility of excess population at the subsistence level of income.

Two treatises by Corden (1971 and 1974) develop the analysis of the way in which the existence of impediments to international trade affects the efficiency of the global economy. This is a somewhat oblique approach to free trade, but it does force the analyst to consider different aspects of various means of interfering with free trade and the consequences of such interference for global welfare. The earlier treatise is predominantly concerned with the introduction of the concept of effective protection to tariff theory. The analysis relies on all the traditional assumptions of international trade theory, except that a multi-state process is needed for internationally-tradable goods. The analysis is static, uses partial and general equilibrium and assumes levels of economic activity to be given. There is always, then, an alternative occupation for any worker displaced by imports. Corden's second book (1974) is much more policy-oriented in its stance, and examines the potential of intervention in international markets for goods. Such action, if it has 'side-effects', is second-best to the elimination of the distortion at its source. The problem of optimal intervention is by what counter-interference can the effects of an intractable divergence between marginal private and social costs and values most efficiently be eliminated? In his second book (1974), Corden still relies on all the static, general-equilibrium and partial-equilibrium analytic frameworks of international trade theory and the economics of welfare. While the assumptions which underlie Corden's analysis are inevitably very restrictive, Corden recognises some of the limitations of his approach (1971, p. 243).

Not all the proponents of unqualified free trade rest their arguments on narrow considerations of economic efficiency. Some people find that a decentralized system of markets with minimal governmental interference has an innate philosophical appeal, and they approach free trade from this philosophic position. One of these is Krauss. Krauss's purpose (1978) is to identify problems that follow from the coexistence of free-market states and welfare states, and the widespread interventionism of welfare states in industries which are involved in international trade. As a preamble to his ultimate inquiry, Krauss reviews what he calls the 'new protectionism' and the argument for free trade. Despite the fact that his book is aimed at non-economists, the argument provides an interesting analysis of how 'free-marketeers' approach the doctrine of free trade. It is not surprising that this variant approach does not probe for any weaknesses of the free trade doctrine, which arise from the assumptions underlying the analysis.

The argument for foreign trade, and by extension for free trade, is explained by means of a $2 \times 2 \times 2$ model of general, static equilibrium. The argument for free trade is based on the benefits derived for the overall economy in constrast to those derived by certain groups from protectionist policies.

The conflict between the economic interests of specific groups within the community, and the economic interests of the community as a whole is the essence of the free trade versus protectionism controversy. Free traders argue from the standpoint of the overall economy, protectionists argue from the standpoint of particular interest groups. (Krauss, 1978, p. 6)

In his enthusiasm for a system of perfectly free markets, Krauss takes positions which surpass those to which many died-in-the-wool free-traders would aspire. He seems to support complete freedom of entry for guest workers and their families (Krauss, 1978, pp. 46-7), and thereby exceeds the commitment of either Henry Simons or Milton Friedman (Reder, 1982, p. 30). Contemplating the possibility of predatory dumping, he argues for complete passivity by the authorities in the importing country because of the (perceived) likelihood that what is seen as predatory dumping is, in fact, permanent dumping. The shift in the terms of trade which accompany dumping is seen to be permanent, and the prices of imports will not be raised when the domestic industry has been driven from the market (Krauss, 1978). In this, Krauss ignores the possibility recognised by Adam Smith (1976, p. 145) that collusion among suppliers is easier when a market is dominated by firms of a single nation. Krauss (1978, pp. 61–8) does not entirely avoid the issue of adjustment to new conditions. He seems to conclude that laissez-faire is the only way by which adjustment can be accomplished. All other approaches are self-defeating or ineffectual. Unemployment insurance is likely to impede workers' geographical mobility, and phase-out policies are recognised as failures on the grounds that they seldom succeed in phasing out the protected industry, but rather get transmuted into rejuvenation policies. The experience in Europe, particularly that of the steel industry (Walter, 1979, and Curzon Price, 1981) indicates the problems inherent in trying to rejuvenate industries by setting severe import limits and cartelising the protected industry. Even such politically-enlightened policies, which are designed to enhance the effectiveness of the free-market system by improving internal job mobility of labour, are denigrated as ineffectual on the basis of the Swedish experience with retraining programmes.

The new protectionism refers to the effects on international trade of the totality of governmental economic measures (compare Blackhurst, 1981). The new protectionism is, then, an outcome of the interventionist philosophies of welfare states (and states with lesser tendencies to intervene in economic phenomena). This intervention encompasses a wide range of policy measures which may increase the international (price) competitiveness of a home industry to reduce imports or to increase exports of a particular good or goods. The problem which exists between welfare and free-market states in international trade policy falls mainly on the free-market state. If the welfare state chooses to influence the prices of tradable goods in its markets, then the free-market state must either compromise its integrity by levying countervailing duties and subsidies, or preserve its integrity by accepting any damage to the interests of some of its members. Surprisingly, Krauss fails to point out that the damage to the free-market economy may not be great, and under the terms of his analysis, could easily result in a gain for all members of the free-market economy. The crucial matter here is the net impact of the export subsidy paid by the welfare state and its import duty on the net barter terms of trade between the two countries. If the joint intervention shifts the terms of trade in favour of the free market economy (the subsidy effect outweighs the tariff's impact), there is a strong probability that everyone in the free-market economy will gain. Krauss's model is one of a smoothly-functioning market system populated by homogeneous factors of production. The only damage that can occur to the free-market economy in the face of a favourable shift in its terms of trade will be felt by those factors who, in the final equilibrium, will have lost relative shares of output and any costs of adjustment through unemployment. If adjustment is rapid, then the latter possibility is quite small and could be outweighed by better real incomes after adjustment. If the elasticity of substitution among factors is high, then even the losing factor will lose only very small amounts of buying power in terms of domestic value added, and the terms-of-trade gain can easily offset such a small loss. This point is merely an application of the Metzler criticism of the Stolper-Samuelson theorem (see Caves, 1960, pp. 70–1).

This variant version of the benefits of a total commitment to free trade, like that of the formal economic model, seems to avoid all the difficult questions posed by reality. Not only are the assumptions about economic conditions idealistic, but the analysis is myopic in the sense that it ignores all matters which are not narrowly economic. This is not to say that free trade and reliance on a smoothly functioning system of markets (if such there be) may not be an optimum economic policy for individual nations as well as for the world. The evidence marshalled by Krauss suggests that the problem with something other than free trade is that governments have no determination to carry out needed measures: that is why laissez-faire is the only effective means of accomplishing a reallocation of factors of production. If the political system is frail to the point of ineptitude, the argument may be valid, but the policy could still inflict heavy social costs during the period of adjustment. Optimality is a relative concept. If political intervention in the economic system is consistently perverse and/or ineffectual, there is no argument for any government intervention whatsoever, and even Adam Smith's minimal role for the state must be dispensed with. This seems extreme, and proponents of pure laissez-passer in international markets must, it seems, provide some measure of the limits of a positive government role.

The equity considerations of free-trade argument are also a matter of concern. The division of total output within a country cannot be too unequal or the self-regulating system may collapse into revolution and anarchy. Economists cannot myopically pursue economic goals without considering the propensity to overthrow the government (I owe that expression to Richard E. Caves). Perhaps both schools will resolve income-distributional problems by means of a transfer mechanism from the gainers to the losers. Such a remedy is certainly implicit in all the more formal approaches based on welfare economics. But if the transfer must be made *among nations,* substantial obstacles may be realised in democratic societies. Hager (1982) introduces the domestic income–distributional problems which follow a change in international trading conditions. He argues that the renunciation of an achieved and equitable distribution of the national product cannot be sacrificed without major social (political) disruption. The problem with viewing the argument for free trade purely in terms of allocative efficiency and world welfare, whatever the measure, is that is abstracts from other social dimensions which may inflict costs that far outweigh the gains. President Ronald Reagan even went so far as to characterise restrictions on trade as threats to peace, and his Special Trade Representative related contemporary problems to the thirties (*New York Times,* 21 November 1982).

There is no need for surprise a the degree of commitment to free-trade policies of economists such as Krauss and Curzon Price (1981, p. 26), both of whom have a fierce attachment to the ideal of individual freedom and to the role of decentralised markets in realising that ideal. The fervour of the commitment of other economists, who are generally not philosophically adverse to interventionist policies by government, is surprising in the light of the restrictiveness of the assumptions which underlie the theoretical base for the argument and narrow its relevance. It is possible, as noted above, that the fervour may derive from the disastrous experience of the thirties when widespread protectionism turned an already intolerable economic situation into something still worse. A more probable reason for the degree of commitment of those 'other' economists may be the perceived fact that most existing examples of protectionism work against their generally accepted criteria of efficiency and equity. In terms of optimal intervention theory, these other economists may see protection as being used to prevent the eradication of a domestic distortion rather than to offset an imperfection. When a union enjoys a wage premium, for example (see Appendix A), it is possible that the bargaining strength of that union will be eradicated by foreign competition. When that happens, the institution of a protective tariff or other device will preserve the union's premium at the expense of efficiency. Since the union is unlikely to have been able to enjoy a wage premium without some monopoly power, the tariff will also offend any criterion for equity. Even allowing for the normative judgments inherent in the equity criteria, there is little reason to question the legitimacy of the antipathy for protection *within the confines of their models*. But these 'other economists' are locked into the analytic framework of the neoclassical theory of international trade, and into its assumptions. These they seem to disregard or downplay. With the exception of some analyses of labour–market congestion, in which most international economists take no part (see Parsons, 1980), the question of the speed of adjustment and the possibility of reducing the social costs of adjustment are overwhelmed by fears of the introduction of everlasting protection. Nor do the other economists question the legitimacy of the assumption that the system can find a job for every worker, provided that aggregate demand is sufficiently stimulated, even though most would be prepared to countenance the existence of surplus labour in many developing nations. There seems to be a sort of Say's Law applied to labour markets so that the free trade solution is necessarily compatible with full employment; that the supply of each level of labour skill creates its own demand for that skill level (within a reasonable period of time).

CONCLUSION

The purpose of this chapter has been to lay the groundwork for criticisms of a total commitment to the free-trade doctrine by presenting in summary form the theories on which the free-trade doctrine rests, and the assumptions that underlie and constrain those theories. The assumptions do impose serious limitations on the basis of the doctrine. The development of the theory of second-best has resulted in a variant on the free-trade doctrine being established. This variant, incorporated by Meade in the concept of 'modified free trade', suggests that imperfections in national markets or in international markets can be offset by explicit interventions by government, and that under certain circumstances these interventions could involve departures from free trade. The practicality of such intervention has been questioned on the grounds that governments (civil servants) are not capable of the fine distinctions and delicate touches necessary for the task.

The concept of optimal intervention is not irrelevant to the purpose of this book. Optimal intervention implies a divergence between social and private marginal costs and values because of some feature of the world. If the imperfection can be countered directly, such a policy is to be preferred. If the imperfection cannot be countered directly, or is intractable to direct measures, trade policies could constitute a second-best approach. A disturbance, or a change in underlying conditions, can be considered an imperfection in the sense that it upsets the existing equilibrium. This book is concerned with the consequences of disturbances of this kind which violate the assumptions of static, general-equilibrium analyses, and with the question of whether or not international trade policies might not constitute the optimal intervention policy. The desirability of using policies which affect international markets depends upon the existence, availability and costs of other options. This task also requires that some of the severely simplifying assumptions used, for example, in Corden's analytic framework must also be discarded. The recognition of factor heterogeneity and the recognition of the existence of inadequate employment opportunities in the short run will necessarily complicate the analysis. As a result, the tidiness that characterises neoclassical theory in international trade will be lost. As Canterbery (1979, p. 19) observes in his development of a complex system of compartmentalised labour markets (see Appendix A); 'the vita theory points toward a structural view of labor demand ... In describing such a process, we lose the determinism of the neoclassical labour market but gain some realism'.

In all this, it is necessary to recognise and to consider the question of the efficiency of policymakers. Many international economists espouse the free-trade doctrine because they accept the formal welfare arguments in its favour, *and* because they question the ability of policy makers to have the conviction and courage necessary for making some of the more complex policy options effective. The policy makers must be able to, and be prepared to, terminate protection for industries given phase-out protection. They must also be prepared to vote the funds needed for positive manpower policies (OECD, 1979). Dyed-in-the-wool free-traders posit that the political system does not allow for the termination of protection, and that the strength of the protected industries (and of their associates) will result in temporary protection becoming permanent. This is a valid criticism of all discretionary policy intervention. This may be true, but politicians have not been educated in the economic theory of adjustment because traditional economics has emphasised the ultimate equilibrium, and not the approach to that equilibrium. Political weakness is not impossible, but no politician can reasonably be expected to legislate efficient policies for adjustment-through-time (if they are possible) when no one supplies a logical framework to support such policies, and with which a politician may fend off the pleas and pressures of interested parties. It is a vicious circle. Economists do not believe politicians are courageous enough to absorb the lesson so economists do not educate politicians so that the logical foundation for courageous action is available.

3 'Domestic Inefficiency' and Conditional Protection

Meade's assumption that the domestic economy operates under conditions which he defined as 'modified laissez-faire' does not reflect reality. Probably one the greatest weaknesses of neoclassical economic analysis is its assumption that competition is effective and pervasive, so that output is produced with minimum inputs and/or at minimum cost. In terms of the traditional argument for free trade, this failing would not be important, since foreign competition will presumably always have a beneficial effect on any imperfections which exist in the domestic economy. For example, a domestic monopoly can only be weakened, and its distorting effect only reduced, by foreign competition. In addition to the assumption of modified laissez-faire, Meade's analysis, like all those cited in the preceding chapter, is set in static equilibrium so that historical time is not allowed to intrude upon the analysis. The exclusion of historical time effectively excludes the possibility of reversible disturbances from the set of conditions to which the free-trade argument applies.

This chapter develops the concept of 'domestic inefficiency' to denote the range and extent of departures from Meade's idealised condition of modified laissez-faire. The possibility that some of the dimensions of domestic inefficiency may be subject to transitory disturbances is reviewed, and the question of the appropriate means of dealing with such disturbances is considered. In particular, the argument for *conditional protection* is considered. Conditional protection would constitute an offer by the government of temporary protection to an industry facing severe import competition, if there existed a logical argument for its protection (such as one of the arguments considered in Chapter 4 below). The members of the industry would commit themselves to reduce or eliminate sources of domestic inefficiency identified in their industry. The award of protection would be conditional on these measures actually being taken.

Section I considers the concept of domestic inefficiency and its application to international competitiveness. Section II then shows how conditional protection might be used in the event of reversible disturbances, and contrasts the concept of conditional protection with straightforward protection or free trade under the existing conditions.[1]

I DOMESTIC EFFICIENCY

Define an industry as being domestically-efficient when it sells its output at minimum feasible money costs of production. This performance is effectively equivalent to that in which a neoclassical firm is a member of an industry in long-run equilibrium in the presence of perfect factor markets. The firms in the industry will earn an adequate rate of return on invested capital, and will sell at the price which equals marginal (and average) long-run costs, including the return on invested capital. This definition serves as a benchmark, and departures from that benchmark are measured by the 'degree of domestic inefficiency' defined as the percentage difference between actual and theoretical minimum costs and prices. A firm enjoying a quasi-rent in the short-run, in response to an increase in industry demand, is technically domestically inefficient. Greater interest centres on distortions which have their origin in supply conditions. Excluding government regulations, which are explicitly oriented toward international markets such as an export duty or some pure non-tariff barriers levied on an import, there are five categories of distortions which can give rise to domestic inefficiency: government regulations which restrict the means of production employed, imperfections in product markets, imperfections in factor markets, impediments placed on the importation of inputs, and X-inefficiency (Leibenstein, 1978). In a two-country model of international trade, what matters is the difference in the degree of domestic inefficiency in an industry in the two countries. Any distortion which has an equal effect on costs in both countries will not affect the pattern of international trade directly.

Government restrictions on the freedom of an industry to use the least-cost combination of inputs can, undoubtedly, arise out of good intentions. Safety regulations can affect costs by reducing the efficiency of an input relative to its unregulated productivity. If the introduction of safety regulations does reduce wages and other costs as a danger premium is eliminated, it is possible that no increase in total costs will result. Alternatively, safety can increase and factors, particularly labour, may continue to receive a traditional hierarchical pay differential relative to a 'safe' industry. Environmental protection measures can be another source of domestic inefficiency if different means of financing the inherent costs are used in two trading partners. When a government requires a firm or industry to employ cost-enhancing procedures to reduce the despoliation of otherwise free resources, the government is determining a price for that input, and the input enters into the cost function of the industry. The price may vary among countries in accordance with the value placed on the cleanliness of the resource. Such procedures do not constitute a departure from domestic efficiency (Gray, 1976b: provided, of course, that the same price is charged to all industries). But for the process to be neutral with respect to international trade, the costs must be passed forward to the ultimate user of the product in accordance with the Polluter Pays Principle (see Barde, 1976). The Polluter Pays Principle (PPP) has been adopted by the OECD on the basis of its trade neutrality (OECD, 1972):

> This principle means that the polluter should bear the expenses of carrying out the above-mentioned measures decided by public authorities to ensure that the environment is in an acceptable state. In other words, the costs of these measures should be reflected in the cost of goods and services which cause pollution in production and/or consumption. Such measures should not be accompanied by subsidies that would create significant distortions in international trade and investment.

If the costs of pollution control do not reflect the values placed on clean resources, and/or are not passed on to the ultimate consumer, a nation can achieve a competitive advantage in international trade in some of its industries by effectively subsidising the cost of an input. If a government decides to assess its industries for damage done to clean resources, and to insist on a reduction in the level of pollution, the cost is either passed forward as in PPP or the necessary equipment can be provided at a subsidised cost, and the costs of operation given special tax treatment so that it is the government and not the ultimate user which bears the cost of the tax. When the ultimate user is a foreigner, trade patterns are distorted. A country obeying PPP will be at a competitive disadvantage (and its industry will be domestically inefficient) relative to the country subsidising pollution removal. In practice, a great many of the less transparent non-tariff barriers will be sources of domestic inefficiency abroad.

Imperfections in product markets are straightforward. Any monopoly will sell its goods at a higher price than an equivalent competitive industry in the absence of effective foreign competition. Monopoly is, then, a source of domestic inefficiency. Note that a monopolist, which enjoys an underlying comparative advantage, could attempt to sell abroad, but it would then commit the sin of 'dumping' by selling abroad at a lower price (adjusted for cost differentials in serving the two markets) than at home. In following such a policy, the firm would run the risk of drawing attention to its monopoly position if the foreign nation (industry) charged the firm with dumping.

Imperfections in factor markets are important in determining the location of some industries, particularly so when the costs of transportation of the product are significantly less than those of a natural resource input. Domestic inefficiency becomes relevant when a country is a member of a cartel, and makes the natural resource available domestically at significantly less than the world (cartel) price. When domestic production of a good is subsidised by means of an effective subsidy being given to an important input, the location of the industry is strongly influenced toward the subsidising country. If the only imperfection in world markets is the cartel, then the relocation of production is merely an example of optimum intervention policy. The effect of the cartel is offset in international trade in downstream manufactures. However, if the necessary cooperating inputs are not available locally, and must be brought to the country subsidising the natural resource input, the subsidy could worsen the efficiency of the system. The international movement of factors is not costless, and to attract these factors additional subsidies may be needed. The problem would be solved by a decentralised system of markets in that corporations would not relocate the cooperating factors unless that cost was exceeded by the cost saving gained from the subsidy of the natural resource. If the cooperating factors are also subsidised, a third-best solution seems probable. In a world of multinational corporations and internationally-mobile proprietary technology, the absence of subsidy of the cooperating factors (so-called investment incentives) is unlikely (see Gray and

Walter, 1983).

The most important imperfection in factor markets, particularly in industrialised (or rich) nations, is the existence of a 'wage premium' paid to workers in an industry as a result of a labour union's control over entry into the industry-specific labour market (see Appendix A). A wage premium inevitably raises the costs of an industry above their theoretical minimum, and makes the industry vulnerable to future changes in industry competitiveness if the wage-premium is slow to react to changed circumstances. Usually, a monopoly position in the factor market relies on the existence of a monopoly or oligopoly position for the industry in the product market. International trade serves as a means of weakening both monopolies, one directly and one indirectly.[2] When unions are sector- rather than industry-specific (if the same union represented workers in the coal, oil and natural gas industries, for example), competition in the product market is still further reduced, and the potential for domestic-*in*efficiency is enhanced. On the other hand, distortions are likely to be smaller in countries such as Japan, where unions are organised and wage negotiations are conducted at an enterprise level. In the absence of collusion among enterprise unions within an industry or sector, greater domestic efficiency may be expected, and any wage premium will be lower (Japanese Institute of Labour, 1979, ch. 2).

Restrictions on imports of intermediate products are also sources of domestic inefficiency. They merit being distinguished from imperfections in domestic factor markets because they are deliberately incurred by governments. Like all imperfections in input-markets, they have effects similar to those analysed in the literature on the effective rate of protection. Any imperfection in an input-market effectively levies a tax on downstream industries and consumers of the final product. It makes no difference whether the 'tax' is imposed by a producers' cartel, by a monopoly union or by government.

The final source of domestic inefficiency is Leibenstein's concept of X-*in*efficiency (1978 and 1979). A firm is deemed to be X-efficient when it achieves minimal feasible costs of production at given factor prices. The degree of X-*in*efficiency is defined as 'the excess of actual over minimum costs for a given output' (Leibenstein, 1978, p. 328). The focal point of theory is that all individuals in a firm do not achieve the utmost in terms of effort and cohesion. Pressures to achieve full effort are self-imposed or are imposed by discipline from management or peer groups. If a firm is operating in an extremely competitive setting, it will be forced to be X-efficient as a condition for survival, but any laxness in the cost-containing forces can lead to less than full effort and cohesion, that is, X-*in*efficiency. Corden (1974) identifies X-efficiency with managerial effort and suggests that X-efficiency will tend to decline in the absence of import competition, therefore protection may lead to inadequate managerial effort. This is a narrow version of a much more complex phenomenon. Different national managerial systems, what Tsurumi and Tsurumi (1984) call 'institution-related technology', can also be a source of X-*in*efficiency and can contribute to a comparative-cost disadvantage in much the same way as do differences in factor endowments.

X-*in*efficiency clearly operates in the same dimension as imperfections in input markets or government regulation. If workers do not achieve maximum efficiency because of industry-wide restrictive work practices, that is an example of X-*in*efficiency deriving from a factor-market imperfection. Had the union chosen to exercise its monopoly power solely in terms of wage-rates, X-efficiency need not be impaired. The distinction between X-inefficiency and other sources of domestic inefficiency is important: under the usual assumption of full employment, the existence of a wage premium affects total output only by means of a change in the output mix. X-*in*efficiency, in contrast, results in less total output. A concrete example of differences in X-efficiency may be seen from the behaviour of two similar plants belonging to the Ford Motor Company. According to Rattner (1981), the Ford plant in West Germany produces 1200 cars per day with 7762 workers while its English counterpart, which has virtually identical equipment, produces only 800 cars per day with 10 040 workers. There will be some difference in wage-rates in the two countries which will counter this difference, so that in the absence of barriers to international trade no international trade in Ford motor cars would take place between the two countries. If the British automobile market is protected from the German industry by some tariff, the workers at Ford in England are enjoying a kind of monopoly (inefficient) rent at the expense of their compatriots.[3]

It is possible that differences in domestic efficiency are societal in origin. To some degree this is true. Managerial practices are frequently peculiar to a nation, and derive originally from culture and geography. The Japanese edge in institution-related technology that currently exists, is societal or cultural in origin, as was the advantage that belonged to American corporations with their multiplant experience in the fifties (Servan-Schreiber, 1969). The general degree of acceptance of governmental regulation of business is also likely to be national. However, the wide range of features that determine an industry's characteristics (capital-intensity, magnitude and economies of scale and labour-relations among others) suggests that societal influences play a small role in the determination of total domestic efficiency.[4]

Domestic efficiency can be defined as the reduction in the costs of production of a particular good relative to a trading partner's industry by virtue of differences in costs not associated with factor endowments. As such, the concept can embrace a multitude of variables in addition to those identified above. Some of these should be identified separately: proprietary technology owned by a firm in one country; experience in product design; the availability of economies of scale as a result of the size of the home market. But domestic inefficiency can result from trade-oriented government action as well as from industry characteristics; overt or covert subsidies paid to foreign firms by their governments are obvious examples.

This chapter is concerned with the interrelation between variations in domestic efficiency and commercial policy. It is analytically useful to begin by taking the level of each as given, and deducing the implications for the other dimension. Then the possible implications of interaction between the two dimensions can be considered. When the level of protection is given, firms may, provided they are not completely constrained by the severity of domestic competition within the industry, allow both prices and costs to drift up to the level permitted by the landed cost of foreign goods. The actuality will depend directly upon the degree of competition within the domestic industry at various levels: inter-firm competition may keep the mark-up rates of the industry virtually constant, but it will not prevent costs from increasing if labour-bargaining takes place on an industry-wide basis. Whether the gains in real income will be taken in increases in wage rates and fringe benefits, or in restrictive work rules and reduced productivity, X-*in*efficiency, cannot be determined despite the different connotations for total output.

The implications can be quickly seen with the aid of the traditional, partial-equilibrium diagram of the effects of a tariff (Figure 3.1). Here the free-trade solution is for the domestic industry to produce OA at price p. The introduction of a tariff at rate t will increase domestic output by AB, and the domestic price to $(p + t)$. If firms within the industry were to react to the introduction of the tariff by allowing their domestic efficiency to decrease, the supply schedule of the domestic industry will shift upwards to S_D', and the domestic rate of output will remain OA. (As noted, the immediate cause of the upward shift in the domestic supply schedule – X-*in*efficiency or other –cannot be identified.) In practice, it seems probable that actual output will fall between A and B, and the extreme results pictured in Figure 3.1 are unlikely eventualities.

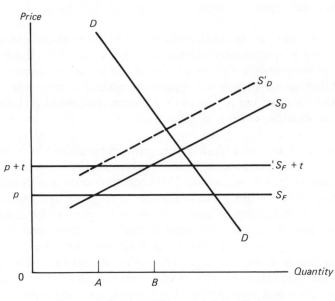

FIGURE 3.1   *A tariff in partial equilibrium*

When an industry is domestically-inefficient and under severe price competition from imports, it will appeal or lobby for import protection (see Appendix B for a report of US procedures for such appeals). In terms of Figure 3.1, the problem can be analysed in terms of a spontaneous downward shift in foreign prices from $(p + t)$ to p (indicating a decrease of t in foreign supply prices). The domestic industry must either contract output by AB (and AB approaches total output as the elasticity of domestic supply approaches infinity), must improve its domestic efficiency by t pence per unit or must generate a further increase in protection in the amount of t, if it is to restore its original rate of output. This is a clear example of the way in which foreign competition will discipline an industry to prevent domestic efficiency or to enforce domestic efficiency in the absence of protection. The whole concept of domestic efficiency constitutes a powerful additional argument against protection (Corden, 1974, and Leibenstein, 1979).

There is, of course, a danger that protectionism will generate domestic inefficiency, and that this will feed upon itself to require more protection. In this context an observation by Barry Bosworth, director of the Council on Wage and Price Stability in the US from 1977–9, is pertinent:

> The economist always says: Well, you'd better restrain your wage increases or your share of the market is going to shrink. But if you talk to these people – on both sides of the bargaining table – you find they have a much better suggestion, which is to march down to Washington and see if they can't get some restrictions on imports (*Fortune,* 20 Sept. 1982, p. 99).

If protection is seen as a feasible alternative to reductions in domestic inefficiency then the damage, which is potentially done by pandering to an industry, can be important. This constitutes what may be termed a 'demonstration effect', and one granting of protection can easily induce other industries to appeal to the authorities rather than to consider their own domestic inefficiencies. A recent issue is the protection of so-called 'hog' motorcycles by the Reagan Administration in the US. The capitulation of the authorities to a small local industry that is clearly and completely non-competitive in terms of price and quality cannot but encourage other industries to follow its precept.[5].

One source of domestic inefficiency which has not been considered so far is the reliability of the product. Undue variation in the reliability of an experience good (one which has to be used for its quality to become manifest) weakens the appeal of the product. A higher proportion of unsatisfactory products can cause a firm to lose its market share. While it is possible for price to offset reduction in reliability to some degree, it would be surprising if that ability were complete, and still more surprising if an industry or a firm which could not maintain good controls over the quality of product would be in a position to engender cost reductions. A deterioration in quality is the result of X-*in*efficiency measured in terms of quality of output rather than in terms of Leibenstein's measure of quantity of output for a given quantity of inputs.

Domestic efficiency or inefficiency is, insofar as it affects commercial policy, a matter of the difference between the departure from minimum costs in both trading partners. Clearly the relative degree of domestic inefficiency must be integrated with the measure of comparative cost advantage arising out of fundamental factors if the direction of trade is to be determined (Gray, 1983). However, the interaction between domestic inefficiency and protection is straightforward. Protection validates domestic inefficiency and domestic inefficiency is likely to generate (successful) pleas for protection. There is a daunting possibility that the two forces may interact so that they are mutually reinforcing.

II THE DYNAMICS OF DOMESTIC INEFFICIENCY AND CONDITIONAL PROTECTION

A disturbance which changes the underlying conditions in a world market can render an industry prey to import competition. From the standpoint of the economy as a whole, a foreign willingness to supply at lower costs can only be favourable. In this section the analysis assumes, for expositional purposes, that all disturbances are adverse from the standpoint of the domestic industry and involve a change in the fundamentals, a decrease in foreign domestic inefficiency or an increase in domestic inefficiency. In this way, the domestic industry will always be the one which has to undergo contraction or find some way to prevent that contraction.

There is an appealing logic in the assertion that severe competitive pressure from imports and domestic inefficiency cannot coexist. Unfortunately this is not so. While the propensity to become domestically inefficient is less when an industry is under severe competitive pressure from imports, some industries do fly in the face of apparent rationality. Often domestic inefficiency and import pressure coexist because of changed conditions over time: the inefficiency has established itself in years when import pressure was negligible or non-existent, and then the underlying conditions have changed adversely so that the domestic industry is now exposed to a much more competitive foreign industry. Rather than attempt to increase domestic efficiency, a firm or industry will frequently seek some alternative. That alternative can be to lobby for protection and/or to complain of the inequity of fate. The next task is to document this problem with particular reference to the US automotive and steel industries.

For an industry to attempt to increase its domestic inefficiency, when the industry is under pressure from imports, is to give apparent contradiction to neoclassical economic theory. The most usual source of such behaviour is an industry-wide labour union, which will attempt to force wage increases through even though it may mean losses for its corporations and reduced employment, at least in the long run. Such a policy may appear more rational in the light of the politics of union democracy. Officers of unions are elected at regular intervals, and any failure to gain an increase in real wage-rates and/or better working conditions can generate an opposition slate of candidates for the incumbents. Therefore union officials are under continuing pressure to show their accomplishments in a positive light, and they develop very short-run horizons. This short-run horizon is probably not incompatible with the thinking of union members, each of whom has a finite employment expectancy. Union officials are thus not unduly concerned about a decrease in employment as long as the rate of employment is less than the expected rate of attrition of union membership through retirement, or even somewhat in excess of this rate. The rank and file of the union will be content even if there is no prospect of enlarged membership. Under conditions such as these, a union may force a wage increase through with the certainty that the increase in labour costs will allow imports to gain a larger share of the domestic market, and will lead to the substitution of labour-saving capital equipment in such plants as remain open. A classic example of such behaviour is that of the United Steel Workers and the steel industry in the US. Table 3.1 shows how real wages in the industry increased absolutely, and relative to 'all manufacturing' during a period in which the ratio of imports to domestic production has risen steadily. At the same time, the steel industry was not earning an adequate rate of return on capital (Crandall, 1981, p. 29). The problem of the return on equity in the steel industry reached the point that the president of the third largest steel producer in the US argued that there was no way by which the US steel industry could hope to raise capital with which to modernise their equipment (Love, 1981). Despite the obvious gains made by the Japanese steel industry, and the growing lack of competitiveness of the US industry, wages in the US industry advanced steadily. Between 1970 and 1976, the Japanese cost per man-hour of labour grew from $1.69 to $5.25 – by $3.56 per hour. The US cost of man-labour increased from $6.10 to $12.14, or by $6.04 per hour (Crandall, 1981, pp. 169–70: the source of these data

TABLE 3.1 *Labour costs in steel and import penetration*

Year	Nominal average hourly earnings ($)	Real average hourly earnings ($) (1967 = 100)	Imports: domestic output (per cent)	Average hourly earnings relative to 'all manufacturing' ($)
1961	3.20	3.57	3.3	1.38
1962	3.29	3.63	4.2	1.38
1963	3.36	3.66	5.0	1.37
1964	3.41	3.67	5.0	1.35
1965	3.46	3.66	7.9	1.33
1966	3.58	3.68	8.1	1.32
1967	3.62	3.62	9.0	1.28
1968	3.82	3.67	13.7	1.27
1969	4.09	3.72	9.9*	1.26
1970	4.22	3.63	10.2*	1.26
1971	4.57	3.77	15.2*	1.28
1972	5.15	4.11	13.3*	1.35
1973	5.56	4.18	12.4*	1.37
1974	6.38	4.32	13.4*	1.45
1975	7.11	4.40	13.5	1.48
1976	7.86	4.61	14.1	1.51
1977	8.67	4.78	17.8	1.54
1978	9.70	4.97	18.1	1.57
1979	10.77	4.95	15.2†	1.61
1980	11.84	4.79	16.3†	1.63
1981	13.11	4.81	18.9†	1.64
1982	13.96	4.83	21.8	1.64

* Voluntary restraint agreements in force.
† Trigger price mechanism in force for the full year.

SOURCES Bureau of Labor Statistics, American Iron and Steel Institute and Robert W. Crandall (1981).

differs from that used in Table 3.1). Although the percentage increase enjoyed by the Americans was smaller, the difference in the base was sufficient to bring about an absolute increase in the difference between wage rates in Japan and the US. This fact, coupled with a significant relative increase in the cost of iron ore, resulted in large increases in the price of US steel relative to Japanese steel. Using hot-rolled steel sheet as a basis for comparison, the cost of the product was about equal in the two countries in 1958 at $66 per short ton. The US industry was protected by a small tariff and by transportation costs. In 1976 the cost of hot-rolled steel sheet in Japan was $121, and in the

US was $175 per short ton (Crandall, 1981, pp. 169–72). The changes in the cost of iron ore, and the substantial relative increases in Japanese productivity, can both be seen as changes in underlying conditions (that is, in comparative cost advantage), but the change in money wage-rates is straightforward domestic inefficiency. Presumably the steel industry and the United Steel workers saw the Japanese threat as transient, felt that they could gain protection when the situation became dire (on grounds of national defence, perhaps), or the union was concerned only with the short-run welfare of incumbents and the threat of strike was potentially too damaging for the corporations to risk undergoing.

While it is probably true that the troubles of the US steel industry began in the fifties, the steel industry is a clear example of an industry which lost its competitiveness against imports at the same time as it grew increasingly domestically inefficient. In contrast, the US automobile industry is an example of an industry which became

TABLE 3.2   *Frequency of automobile repair records, by national origin in the US*

Country of origin	Early period †		Later period ‡	
	Raw score §	Average score	Raw score §	Average score
Japan ¶	153/38	4.03	365/86	4.24
Germany	161/46	3.50	204/62	3.29
United States	624/244	2.63	1193/434	2.75
Sweden	27/11	2.45	45/15	3.00

Scale: 5 = much better and 4 = better than average;
3 = average; 2 = worse and 1 = much worse than average

† Model years 1972–5 assessed by questionnaire in 1976.
‡ Model years 1974–9 assessed by questionnaire in 1980.
§ The raw score denotes the total number of points earned and the number of models/years reported. Data for the category 'overall record' only were used.
¶ The improvement in Japanese reliability is due to the improvement in Toyota cars from 3.94 to 4.70: excluding Toyota, the Japanese average score declined slightly from 4.10 to 4.03.

SOURCES: Consumer Union, *Consumer Reports: The 1977 Buying Guide Issue* (Mount Vernon, NY:1976), pp. 375–83, and Consumer Union, *Consumer Reports Buying Guide Issue, 1981* (Mount Vernon, NY: 1980, pp. 378–98.

exposed to foreign competition largely as a result of a very large adverse disturbance, and was not able to increase its domestic efficiency quickly enough to avoid losing a significant share of its domestic market to imports. The oil price shock in 1973 brought about an abrupt change in taste on the part of the US consumer for smaller, more fuel-efficient cars. The US industry was less competitive in that end of the market partly because of the level of wage-rates, and to a smaller degree because of the higher cost of steel in the US. What had been a reasonable cost structure, despite a standard wage-rate well in excess of the national average for production workers (domestic inefficiency), was now made vulnerable by the quality of design and product of foreign carmakers. The US industry came to be known as a producer of unreliable cars (see Table 3.2). Some of the loss of market share by the US industry can be attributed to the slowness of reaction of management which tended to ignore incontrovertible evidence that it had to produce small cars to maintain its market share. This factor, coupled with the domestic inefficiency and unreliability of the product, led the industry to ask for protection, and ultimately to gain a mildly restrictive 'voluntary export restraint' by the Japanese industry.

The US industry has slowly and steadily begun to regain a market share after a period of large losses and high unemployment. Some improvement in domestic efficiency was achieved through reductions in wage-rates (so-called 'givebacks'); designs and quality standards were improved, although casual reading in *Consumer Reports* suggests that the US industry has still not managed to equal the reliability of its Japanese competition. The success of the industry in 1982 and 1983 was achieved despite a severe overvaluation of the US dollar in terms of the yen amounting to, according to some educated guesses, as much as 20 per cent.

The improvement in the performance of the US industry suggests that the loss of market share in the seventies was due to transitory factors, of which management inefficiency and domestic inefficiency caused by the continuation of wage premiums in the industry which the underlying circumstances no longer warranted, were among the more important. Some of the lack of competitiveness was also ascribable to sheer X-*in*efficiency. One case in particular was well reported when Ford closed its production plant in Mahwah, NJ (Carley, 1980). Here absenteeism was inordinately high, worker morale was low to the point that marijuana was smoked on night shifts and the reliability of the product was well below average for

Ford plants in North America. Some of the problems may have arisen because of the cost pressures forced on Ford by high wage-rates and low-priced Japanese competition, but the story of the plant closing is an object lesson in inefficiency. However, workers never seemed to realise that the continued operation of 'their' plant was in doubt. Before it was closed, the plant did greatly improve the quality of its product.

Some indication of the dynamics of union politics and costs in an industry facing severe import competition can be seen from the reaction within the United Auto Workers to the union leadership on the subject of givebacks. The rank-and-file members of the union seemed to hold the union leadership to blame for their having suffered a reduction in their wage premium:

> Most of the current disaffection (with the union leadership) arises from the UAW's flexibility in helping the auto industry struggle through rough times. Union leaders believe that wage and benefit givebacks, the acceptance of plant closings and strengthened cooperation with management have been realistic responses to the industry's troubles. Many once-proud rank-and-file union members, however, believe that such actions indicate that the union has simply become weak and unable – or unwilling – to stand up for their interests. (Buss, 1983)

What seems to be a lack of economic awareness (of potential vulnerability) hinders decreases in domestic inefficiency when import pressure becomes substantial. While these industries provide useful examples of domestic inefficiency in the face of heavy import pressure, the problem is not confined to these industries or to US industries.[6]

International competitiveness comprises a combination of the cost advantage deriving from the existing underlying conditions, plus the net degree of domestic efficiency of the home industry against its foreign competitor. Traditional trade theory considers only the cost advantage or disadvantage stemming from the underlying conditions of factor endowments and tastes. An industry can be internationally competitive, that is, it can avoid imports or exports if its comparative cost advantage exceeds any net domestic inefficiency or if its net domestic efficiency exceeds any comparative cost disadvantage. When underlying conditions change abruptly, and industry relying on its comparative cost advantage to outweigh its net domestic inefficiency will become vulnerable. Given time it may be able to reduce its net domestic inefficiency and compete successfully again, although this does not necessarily imply that the industry will regain its original market share. An adverse disturbance could provide a rationale for temporary protection of an industry which has temporarily lost its competitiveness: what may be termed an 'embattled industry'. An industry can become embattled when (and assuming the domestic efficiency of foreign competitors is unchanging):

(a) a temporary and reversible change in international trading conditions occurs which reduces the industry's comparative cost advantage. (This possibility is best illustrated by a country having an overvalued currency for a short period, due possibly to an inflow of interest-sensitive capital.)

(b) a permanent change in international trading conditions takes place so that the comparative cost advantage previously enjoyed changes to a comparative cost disadvantage (given constant degrees of domestic inefficiency in both countries). There are two possible cases: the (new) cost disadvantage can be smaller than the home country's degree of domestic inefficiency, in which event the industry is capable of reestablishing its international competitiveness; or the new cost advantage exceeds the degree of domestic inefficiency so that the industry must be allowed to die.

(c) a temporary change in domestic efficiency which exceeds the existing margin of comparative advantage.

Any argument for providing temporary protection to embattled industries must be predicated on the fact that a 'hands-off' policy will involve larger total social costs than temporary protection. A crucial aspect of the problem, is, then, the ability of embattled industries to reestablish their international competitiveness in a laissez-faire, free-trade environment.

The authorities have three different courses which they can pursue: a hands-off policy which amounts to an unswerving commitment to free trade, straightforward protection on either a temporary or permanent basis with the positive likelihood that the temporary protection will be prolonged beyond its original limit, and conditional protection.

A hands-off policy runs the risk that the domestic industry will fail before the industry can recover from the disturbance. This possibility is not inconsequential because the needs of an embattled industry for more up-to-date capital goods will be hard to fund. Financial capital is extremely difficult to raise when profits are zero or negligible and there is serious competition from imports. An increase in domestic efficiency may not occur spontaneously, and conditions may have to reach a critical state (possibly beyond 'the point of no return') before the cooperation of labour can be assured.[7] The more set the hierarchical inter-industry pattern of wages, the less likely is cooperation to be available to the embattled industry in the form of wage reductions. There is, then, a significant probability that bankruptcies will occur within the embattled industry with consequent reductions in industry capacity. For new firms to emerge to take the place of the bankrupt organisations will be difficult, particularly in major industries where the optimum firm size is very large. The reaction is asymmetric: it is easier for the capacity of the domestic industry to decline than it is for new capacity to be built. There is a danger that a hands-off policy will limit the domestic industry to a long-run share of the domestic market, which is less than it would be in some long-run equilibrium when the industry has had ample time to recover from the disturbance.

A second facet of the problem is the 'industrial organisation' of the industry after full adjustment has been made. One possibility is that the domestic industry will have been reduced to one giant so that a domestic monopoly exists and which would offer grounds for monopoly rents if the underlying international conditions were to change favourably in the future. A still less attractive outcome is the possibility that the domestic industry will be eliminated, and the foreign suppliers will come from a single country: under such circumstances, one might expect the possibility of collusion among the suppliers of imports to exist, and for the domestic market to be cartelised. Such an eventuality might not be the purpose of establishing the foreign corporations in the domestic market (that is, there is no hint of predatory dumping) but once the market is dominated, collusion could easily become attractive. A simple hands-off approach, such as that implicit in Ambassador Brock's statement, 'the Administration believes companies have the right to fail' (*Forbes,* 8 June 1981, p. 160), may not be an efficient policy unless domestic inefficiency can be wiped out at the wave of a politician's wand.

Unconditional protection, whether ostensibly temporary or granted *sine die,* does not attack any domestic inefficiency which may exist within the industry. Once again the steel and automotive industries of western Europe and North America are the best examples. The automotive industries have been appealing for protection from Japanese imports. In western Europe, the problem of the steel industry is enhanced by ethnic divisiveness in Belgium and by the fact that the steel corporations are, in some countries at least, publicly owned, and the government is involved in the issue in a direct economic as well as a political economic dimension. With the exception of Curzon Price's reference to the recent emergence of conditional assistance in some countries (1980, p. 205), and here the conditions relate to the closing down of outdated capacity, protection has tended to be unconditional and sometimes to consist of an almost invisible network of special arrangements or credits, subventions and non-tariff barriers. One particularly dangerous form of protection to emerge is 'sectoral protection' under which insiders within the industry design and develop, with tacit governmental approval, their own protective measures (Walter, 1979):

> More generally, one can argue strongly that sectoral trade negotiations in themselves pose serious threats for a liberal international trading system. They are too narrow, and almost by definition, too producer-oriented to take more general welfare considerations into account. The asymmetries involved inherently bias the outcomes toward 'arrangements' that are highly distortive of international market conditions, especially in a dynamic sense. And, once such 'arrangements' have been made and anchored in international trade law or precedent, experience shows that they tend to be essentially permanent even after the causative factors are dissolved.

The indirect effects of unconditional protection tend to be overlooked by governments concerned with acquiescing to political pressures from vested interests and concerned with their own financial stakes in the vulnerable industries.

One problem with protection is that it is interdependent. As soon as one industry is protected by its government, overtly or covertly, the governments in other nations are induced to match the degree of protection lest their own industry become vulnerable. Several possible scenarios suggest themselves. One is for the first government to intervene to set a standard for others to emulate. Under these conditions, the industry gains worldwide at the expense of other industries. A second scenario with similar results is for the government which offers the greatest assistance to set the standard by virtue of its being 'high bidder' in terms of its willingness to burden taxpayers in support of the endangered industry. The third scenario is the cartel-like marketing arrangement which Walter sees as a major feature of sectoral protection. Under this schema, the industry agrees on marketing quotas which, coupled with a mass of countervailing tariffs, achieve a complex, bureaucratically-determined means of retaining the capacity of each industry by neutralising changes in international efficiency.

This system deprives the industry of any incentive to improve its domestic efficiency. Unfortunately the process does not seem to be static since the domestic inefficiency seems to increase steadily under these conditions, and ultimately adjustment must be confronted. The adjustment then is made under crisis conditions. A good example of the failure of an industry to reverse its tendency towards domestic inefficiency is the plight of the British Steel Corporation (BSC) in early 1981. The chief executive of BSC threatened to liquidate the company unless wage freezes (decreases in real wage rates), and a reduction in the work force of approximately 15 per cent were agreed by the unions. BSC's output per worker had long been the lowest in Europe, and the difference had not been offset by differences in wage rates (Borders, 1981). Partly because of the plight of BSC, the industry within the European Economic Community (EEC) was at odds with itself and unable to agree on a system by which its steel prices could be made competitive and its excess capacity reduced. Much of the problem within the EEC derived from different levels of domestic efficiency in different member countries.

When countries with vulnerable industries fail to match the degree of protection instituted by others, their own markets become the focus of the export strategy of internationally-efficient producers. Thus protection against imports by, say, France makes efficient producers likely to concentrate their sales in other markets, and in this way the industry that did not receive protection is put under additional strain.

In nations bedevilled by inflation the costs of unconditional protection are fairly self-evident. By protecting an industry without instituting cost–reducing policies, the country loses an opportunity to avail itself of a cost reduction in an important sector. Similarly, by preventing a decrease in the cost of an industrial commodity, the policy inflates the price of 'downstream products', increases the vulnerability of these industries to foreign competition and causes the current account to deteriorate. It is possible that the vulnerability of the US automobile industry to Japanese competition derives, in part, from its disadvantaged position in the purchase of steel.

All these indirect effects of unconditional protection suggest that this policy is likely to be the most attractive to short-sighted politicians, and most damaging to the long-run interests of the economy. It is this policy set which fervent free-traders envisage when they are concerned with the evils of protectionism. Even if the protection is transitory, they presuppose either that the duration of protection will be extended, or that the adjustment will be as severe when it ultimately is enforced as it would be if allowed to happen without the protection being instituted.

There exists a third possible policy which can be described as 'conditional protection'. This policy would grant temporary protection in return for commitments by both management and labour to undertake measures which will increase the domestic efficiency of the industry and its international cost-competitiveness. Curzon Price (1980) reports on the adoption of conditional assistance in the steel industry in western Europe but that policy, involving the scrapping of production units, with no hope of achieving international competitiveness, was born out of *ad hoc* common sense married with desperation rather than from any preconceived and generally-applicable policy stance. The advantage of having conditional protection recognised as a third policy option is that such measures could be more quickly applied to embattled industries, which would have less time to get deeply into trouble before their fate was decided. The schema also has the advantage of instilling into management and labour an understanding of what is involved in seeking protection. It would prevent protection being seen as an easy solution.

The crux of the issue is that the industry is 'embattled', that is it has a high probability of reestablishing its international competitiveness. It is not a senile industry, which cannot reestablish its competitiveness and which would qualify for protection only on a phase-out basis (see Chapter 4 below). Any form of protection will impose costs on consumers in the short run at least. The measures undertaken by management and labour to increase the domestic efficiency of the industry are the *quid pro quo* for the imposition of short-run costs on the consumers. Any protection accorded will be temporary and may be expected to vary inversely with the severity of the commitments undertaken by those in the industry. Leglislation would probably impose a maximum duration for any such protection, and any extension of such protection would constitute phase-out protection, which builds in a diminution of the degree of protection through time.

The actual commercial-policy device used can vary. A subsidy per unit of output produced may be the best since subsidies can be limited to plants and firms which are identified as embattled rather than senile, and because subsidies if they are funded without real costs, are recognised as being a preferable tool of commercial policy, do not distort the relative prices facing users and are potentially compatible with optimal intervention (Bhagwati and Ramaswami, 1963). Fiscal realities make a tariff or a quota a more probable means of protection.

The commitments to reduce domestic inefficiency come from both management and labour, and the protection would be revoked if these commitments were renounced. Labour and salaried workers recognise that their rates of pay exceed those compatible with the viability of the industry, given the capital stock *in situ,* given the cost of foreign goods and given the effectiveness (X-efficiency) of management. Labour and salaried workers will agree to gradual decreases in their real (inflation-adjusted) wage rates. It will probably be easier to achieve such a commitment in inflationary times when nominal wage-rates could remain constant. Any such changes, which must be gradual rather than abrupt, will be smaller (and potentially even zero) the greater is the agreed reduction in work rules and/or renunciation of fringe benefits. It is not reasonable to expect labour to accept a cut in remuneration without some equivalent action on the part of management. Management's salaries will be reduced in real terms at the same or a higher speed than that agreed to by labour. If need be, both salaries and wage rates can be indexed to value added in manufacturing to guard against excessive, inflation-induced reductions in real wages. No bonuses will be awarded to management, and steps must be taken to ensure that salary increases are given only for *bona fide* promotions. Dividends will not be paid, and any profits made by the firm will be ploughed back into the same industry and factories. Profits must not be reallocated to other endeavours in which a conglomerate may have an interest. Profits will not be used to generate net increases in capacity.

Any complicated schema of this kind runs the risk of being too subtle for the practicalities of a bureaucratic world (see Blackhurst, 1981). It may still be possible to generate conditional protection in a slightly less refined way by requiring that any protection sought by an industry must be accompanied by salary reductions for management and labour of 5 per cent, followed by a freeze for the duration of the protection, and by a prohibition of channelling any profits to uses other than the improvement of the capital stock in the industry. Protection in this vein will not pander to senile plants, nor will it allow X-*in*efficiency to increase. What conditional protection is designed to do is to act as the catalyst which will enable an industry quickly to realize that its dilemma calls for combined action by management and labour and that, the traditional antagonism between management and labour is shelved while the industry is embattled.

The potential subtleties of such a policy package are not the only source of difficulty. The package would have to be ratified by the GATT. There is probably room for policies of this type under the escape clause (Clause XIX), but to the extent that the incorporation of the package into the GATT rules caused difficulties, the policy package would not be available for use unilaterally. One could imagine that the membership of the GATT would want to prescribe limits to the protection involved in order to ensure that the protection was both conditional and transitory. In this sense, the GATT could serve another useful purpose by ensuring that any actions are, in fact, temporary. Action of this kind would also make it unnecessary for nations to meet what are describd as short-run economic problems by resorting to measures which bypass the GATT, such as orderly marketing arrangements and voluntary export restrains.

One of the major difficulties will be the need to distinguish between embattled plants and firms and their senile counterparts. Straightforward cost-accounting procedures should be able to identify clear cases of both kinds, but there will inevitably be borderline cases. Nor is it clear to see how calculations such as would be necessary would be made when a currency is overvalued (a term which itself lacks clear definition). This problem, like virtually all others, is enhanced when the capacity or the industry is owned by the national government: the need for temporary protection cannot but provide a field day for the wit and rhetoric of the government's opposition. The political problems will also be aggravated by what is an apparent conflict between the issues of equity and efficiency. In distinguishing between embattled and senile plants, it is probable that the senile plants will be older, more likely to have older workers and their closure will be associated with larger human costs. Disemployment of older workers is more likely to swell the ranks of the unemployed rather than lead to a change in employment (see Chapter 5 below).

The final problem calls for the wisdom of Solomon: how to recompense workers for their contribution to the survival of the individual firm. The cost to the stockholder of conditional protection is the insistence on having profits ploughed back into the embattled industry, but as long as the firms in that industry do not ultimately fail, the stockholders will find their net worths improved in the long run. Similarly management can be kept in the industry by means of stock options, so that they will be financially rewarded when the firm recovers and is internationally competitive again. Workers forgo their traditional wage rate, and their only reward is to maintain their employment. This fact is not insignificant, but labour unions and human nature will require more. There is no reason in principle why workers could not be offered stock options in an embattled firm in exactly the same way as management. This scheme has the advantage of sharpening the workers' involvement in the undertaking. What this amounts to is a system of profit-sharing for future profits – if such there be.

III SUMMARY

By itself, the identification of the concept of domestic inefficiency and its incorporation into a theory of international trade (Gray, 1983) strengthens rather than weakens the argument for free trade in the traditional static framework. Freer trade and more international competition can only tighten the cost-containing forces which exist in a national economy.

Release of the static assumption allows for the possibility of reversible disturbances by which a firm or an industry can be temporarily unable to compete with foreign firms. When this fact is coupled with the existence of domestic inefficiency, the case for a simple hands-off policy becomes weak, and there is an argument to be made for awarding an embattled industry temporary and conditional protection. In fact, the concept of conditional protection has much to recommend it in quite general terms since the establishment of conditions which would automatically accompany any award of protection might well reduce the alacrity with which firms seek this solution. The task that conditionality performs is to reduce and possibly eliminate the traditional adversary relationship which exists between labour and management in many countries. Since this antagonism will tend to delay the achievement of reductions in domestic inefficiency until some possible crisis enforces cooperation, its early removal cannot but play a positive role in the face of a severe disturbance.

This policy package is not without its inherent difficulties. Foremost among these is the ability of policy makers to distinguish between senile and embattled industries. Equally problematic is the ability of the policy making bureaucracy to cope with the subtleties of the argument. It may be necessary to implement conditional policy in a relatively simple way reminiscent of the Chicago advocacy of a straightforward set of rules for monetary policy, on the grounds that the matter was too complex for a discretionary approach.

4 The Problem of the *Rate* of Adjustment

This chapter addresses the possibility that a nation will incur unnecessarily large social costs in undergoing adjustment to a permanent disturbance at the speed dictated by a laissez-f .ire policy. Adjustment is defined as the reallocation of resources from one industry to another, and may obviously involve spatial relocation as well as inter-sectoral transfer. No country can or should want to completely avoid the social costs of adjustment. When change comes at a measured pace, the costs of adjustment are small relative to the benefits of the growth which they facilitate, and the vitality which adaptability can impart to an economic system. Change is the inevitable companion of economic progress. Even when the disturbance is adverse to the interests of the nation, acceptance of the new international trading conditions will lead to a better long-run economic performance than the suppression, by commercial policy, of the needed adjustment. The international aspect of measured change is best exemplified by the change in comparative advantage of marginal industries as they die out in rich countries and relocate themselves in developing countries (Akamatsu, 1962). Kojima (1973) stresses the role of technology transfer under the *aegis* of multinational corporations in facilitating this kind of adjustment by enhancing the efficiency of the new exporting nation, but this may not eliminate social costs in the rich country as workers find relocation difficult (Gray, 1972, pp. 201–4). The process of adjustment imposes its social cost when the pace of change exceeds that to which the economy can adapt without dislocative unemployment of resources. This is the problem of 'accelerated adjustment' (see Chapter 1 above).

The doctrine of free trade implies a complete passivity in the face of change, so that adjustment will take place at the rate determined by the dictates of uninhibited market forces. Whatever the efficiency of a system of markets as an allocator of resources in times of slow change, it is not clear that it is a perfect, or even satisfactory, mechanism for enforcing change in the face of a disturbance of some magnitude. The OECD (1979) implies that markets fall short of perfect efficiency under such conditions, and identifies two main kinds of intervention: industrial policies, and employment and manpower policies. The latter are 'positive' adjustment policies designed deliberately to facilitate and enhance the capacity for change, while industrial policies are conceived of as 'protective', 'defensive' or 'adjustment-retarding'. Curzon Price (1981) conceives of positive industrial policies, but does not develop the concept, except in a context of conditions being attached to the award of the protective aspects of those same industrial policies. The first condition prescribed by OECD for adjustment to take place with minimal dislocation is for a high level of demand to exist within the adjusting economy, so that job vacancies exist for those workers displaced from industries adversely affected by the change in international conditions. Any adjustment-retarding policies which may have to be introduced to keep social costs within acceptable limits are to be dispensed with as quickly as economic recovery allows. The reader will recall the requirement of a high level of aggregate demand that is built into the theoretical models underlying the free-trade argument. Krueger (1980, p. 245), in a more empirical consideration of the problem, stresses the relationship between social costs and the spontaneous rate of economic growth in the importing country. It may be useful to conceive of the process of adjustment as involving either 'pull' or 'push' forces. When change is induced by spontaneous growth, social costs tend to be small because the high level of aggregate demand is necessarily present. This is a 'pull' disturbance with the high level of demand occurring in the country in which the required reallocation of factors is most substantial. It is also a 'pull' disturbance in foreign countries which feel the effects in the form of an increase in the demand for their exports. It is possible for a 'pull' disturbance to involve accelerated adjustment costs, but these costs are likely to be tempered by the fact that the actual rate of growth achieved will be constrained by the ability of factors to shift from one sector to another. When the originating disturbance is an increase in supply in a foreign country such that, for example, there is a spontaneous shift in the supply of exports, the importing country must react to the new conditions in a context of no (or negligible) growth: the buoyancy of aggregate demand will be lacking. This constitutes a 'push' adjustment with higher likelihood of noteworthy costs of adjustment in the importing country. Only when the world growth rate is high can one expect a change in export capacity not to generate a push-type adjustment in the importing country. Self-evidently the argument for protection as a means of tempering the rate of change is applicable exclusively to push-type adjustments. Many economists seem to have pull-type disturbances in mind when they speak of the beneficial effects of unimpeded international trade in a dynamic context (Walter, 1981–2).

In practice, the assumption of a high level of aggregate demand in the adjusting (or importing) country implies two considerations which may be questioned in a real-world or pragmatic analysis. The ability to maintain high levels of aggregate demand implies an ability successfully to institute so-called Keynesian fine-tuning policies. This has not proved practicable in western economies in recent years of adaptation to real shocks. When high levels of aggregate demand are to be maintained in the face of a change in international trading conditions leading to push adjustment, balance-of-payments considerations may inhibit expansionist domestic macroeconomic policies, unless foreign markets are particularly buoyant *and* open to exports. The secret of successful adjustment lies in the development of policies which increase the capacity of the economy to accept and incorporate change. Employment and manpower policies enhance the mobility of displaced workers by emphasising supply measures, such as training, mobility-enhancing programmes and placement system to facilitate adjustment to shifting demands, technological progress and changing patterns of international trade. Job creation programmes may be targeted more directly to benefit clearly-defined groups encountering problems of structural unemployment. As a part of the improved functioning of the labour market, the OECD calls for less rigidity of wage rates to ensure that 'the structure of wages does not inhibit the adjustment of labour supply to changing needs, and adversely affect the employment prospects of certain types of labour' (OECD, 1979, p. 7).[1] McKersie and Sengenberger (1983) develop the concept of the 'integrative approach' to structural change. This strategy is the antithesis of laissez-faire. It assumes that the government can help the economy to effect a given process of adjustment by increasing the economy's adaptability, and in this way lowers the social costs of adjustment. This strategy involves government interference with the system of markets – mainly through subsidies – to promote the mobility of capital between industries by closing down out-of-date plants, and simultaneously safeguard the jobs of workers in declining industries. All this is designed to make protection against imports unnecessary, and indeed, 'tis a consummation devoutly to be wished'. The focus of McKersie and Sengenberger's study is structural change, and the source of that change is a matter of some indifference.

It is possible to use protection against imports as a means of slowing the pace of change, which can be caused by a domestic disturbance. With the exception of spontaneous increases in domestic *in*efficiency, protection against imports must be expected to be a clumsy way in which to slow down internally-generated change. This chapter focuses on problems which have their origin in the international sector, and it will assume that the domestic efficiency of tradable goods industries is constant at home and abroad. Domestic disturbances will be considered as potential reinforcers of, or offsets to, international disturbances in Section IV.

Any analysis of a process of change must renounce the traditional theory of international trade. Bertil Ohlin (in a personal letter to the author) rejected the notion that his was a general-equilibrium theory of international trade. Instead, Ohlin emphasized that his approach was 'a comparison of different positions with essential comments on the forces of transition from the one to the others. The equation system and equilibria serve only as an introduction!' Ohlin's view does not seem to have permeated the thinking of theorists working in the traditional model of international trade. There are two ways in which a wrenching disturbance in international markets can cause serious dislocation: through market congestion, and by sudden reductions in the capitalised value of human and physical industry-specific capital in industries subjected to increased foreign competitive pressures. Neither process can be understood in a analytic framework confined to long-run equilibria; both need a short-run approach. This chapter relies very heavily for its underlying theory on the vita theory of income distribution developed by E. Ray Canterbery (1979, 1980). This theory is summarised in Appendix A, and readers completely unfamiliar with Canterbery's model may wish to read the appendix first. Section I adapts the notation of the vita theory for the tasks at hand. Section II develops the analysis of factor–market congestion with particular reference to labour. Section III examines the desirability of phase-out protection for senile industries with large amounts of industry-specific physical and human capital. Finally Section IV considers the possibility of extraneous reinforcing disturbances.

I CANTERBERY'S VITA THEORY

Canterbery's vita theory derives its name from the emphasis placed on the life history of an individual in determining that person's skills and other attributes at some point in time. A national supply of labour is characterised by each potential worker being located in a particular place and having a certain set of skills – both general and industry-specific. Because it takes time for a person to change the attributes which he or she brings to the market and to relocate geographically, the supply of labour is determined in the short run by the existing characteristics of the work force. Each separate and identifiable category of skills constitutes a cell in a regional labour market. Movement between two regional labour markets, or between two different cells in the same market, takes time: a person may relocate spatially or acquire new skills, or even downgrade themselves to a labour market which requires a less demanding set of skills. Ideally each worker will seek employment in the highest-paying cell for which he or she is qualified and may, if the reward is sufficient, spend time and financial assets on upgrading the skills which can be offered. If the national supply of labour may be characterised by a matrix of categories of existing skills for each region, with each cell in the matrix showing the number of people qualified for that submarket, so too may the national demand for labour. Given levels of aggregate demand, the demand for workers in a geographic market by general skill level and by industry-specific skill is fixed in the short run. The demand for labour is determined by the physical stock of capital in the various industries, the embodied technology and the mix of goods demanded. Over a period of time, both the pattern of demand and supply may change: demographic changes and changes in the skill level of the population affect the supply matrices, and the demand matrices are changed by alterations in the stock of physical capital in response to new technologies and changes in the relative costs of inputs, and by changes in the mix of goods demanded. Any mismatching between the set of supply and demand matrices indicates 'structural unemployment' (given an adequate level of aggregate demand). This chapter is concerned with the process of adaptation in the demand and supply matrices to changes in the mix of goods demanded. The technology of the stock of physical capital may be assumed constant, and the disturbance identified as a change in the mix of goods demanded as foreign suppliers displace home-country firms in some markets and increase their demand for the output of others. To understand the process of adjustment, it is necessary first to understand the determinants of the supply of labour.

The vita theory stresses the accumulation of human capital by individuals through a combination of birth endowments and the acquisition of skills and credentials. The first components to affect the level of skills acquired are the individual biological inheritance (*G*) and the familial environment (*E*). The actual level of human capital available at some point in time combines the effects of additional training with *G* and *E*. Naturally, the greater the availability of financial capital (*K*) and encouragement (through *E*), the more easily will a person acquire skills. The greater the amount of human capital or skills acquired (*k*), the greater will be the wage rate or salary. While *k* may be considered to apply to levels of human capital acquired, it is also necessary to recognise the existence of product- and industry-specific skills. The national labour force (or the labour force in a region) will be characterised by its distribution among the many cells of the matrix: this distribution will reflect the distribution of birth endowments and social attitudes towards the acquisition of *k*, as well as of the availability of both formal and on-the-job training. Following Canterbery (1979), the process of adjustment can be considered in terms of three kinds of relocation: spatial, temporal and skill–specific. The mobility among job markets (among cells in different regional matrices) involves spatial relocation as the worker (and family) move geographically. Mobility between cells in the same matrix requires temporal relocation as increases in *k* require time or skill-specific relocation as an individual acquires new industry-specific *k* without any increase in the general level of human capital. All three kinds of relocation require withdrawal from the labour force for a period of time at a cost to the individual or the state. (It is possible that a firm will bear the burden by retraining its own workers for new positions within the enterprise.)

An individual's wage-rate is determined by the rate paid to occupants of the highest cell to which the individual may aspire and find employment. The highest cell in the matrix, and therefore the wage-rate, is determined by a large number of variables:

$$W = w\,(k,\ \varkappa,\ \rho,\ m,\ \Theta,\ M,\ R,\ \tau) \qquad (4.1)$$

where $\varkappa$ is non-human capital available, ρ is the price of the end product, m and Θ are, respectively, assessments of the ease of mobility and the uncertainty surrounding the costs and benefits of relocation, M is any monopoly power in the submarket due to either a labour union's or a professional association's ability to create barriers to entry, R is a factor of discrimination and τ represents experience. Both k and τ can be product- or skill-specific, and the other variables are then identified in terms of the relevant k^i and the τ^i. If the relevant k^i or τ^i should lose value, the worker can 'reconstitute' his or her equation (4.1) in terms of the best available k^i or τ^i. For present purposes, equation (4.1) can be condensed to:

$$W = w(k, \rho, m, M) \qquad (4.2)$$
$$k = k(G, E, \varkappa, \tau, s)$$

with m serving to represent both dimensions of mobility, and s the amount of formal education and training which the individual has received. The partial of W with respect to all eight independent variables is positive. The only other partial which can be identified with certainty is $\delta m/\delta k$, which is positive.

The process of adjustment to a change in the pattern of goods demanded and therefore in the derived demand for labour, as a result of an international disturbance, must involve the creation or aggravation of structural unemployment. The social costs of adjustment will be greater, the greater is the amount of unemployment. The crux of the social costs of adjustment is, then, the mechanism by which workers change from the cell in which they have been offering their services to another cell in which excess demand exists. (For simplicity of exposition, attention here is focused on the mix of employment and not on the level: this section assumes that the disturbance will create and destroy an equal number of jobs.) The magnitude of a shock is determined by the amount of structural unemployment which it creates, and the severity of a shock on the degree of temporal and spatial relocation involved in the adjustment process. Given that labour within a single cell in a regional supply matrix is perfectly substitutable, a disturbance which changes the pattern of demand from, say, cars to light trucks or vans, would be a disturbance of negligible concern since virtually no structural employment would be created. For a disturbance of a given magnitude, the severity of the disturbance depends upon the geographic distance between labour markets with the same level of human capital in excess demand and supply, and upon the amount of additional k needed by the displaced workers to be able to qualify for the cells in which excess demand exists.

Faced with unemployment in their own labour market (the cell in the regional matrix), workers have an incentive to relocate geographically and/or to retool to make themselves suitable for the alternative employment vacancies which exist. If the prospect of being rehired in the original cell is good, workers will tend to sit out the period of unemployment as best they can rather than to relocate either temporally or spatially. If the prospects for being rehired are not good, workers need information about the location in which jobs are available and on the kinds of skills needed; both require information, time and money. The ability to spend money on either form of relocation will depend on the availability of money, and on the assessment of the probabilities that the vacancy will still be vacant when the relocation has been accomplished. This process is going on continually as normal change takes place. Sometimes these changes are accomplished intergenerationally, but workers always have an incentive to acquire k if the expected return exceeds the costs. If the cost, in terms of a reduction in income (through unemployment and the costs of relocation), exceeds the expected net benefit, a displaced worker will downgrade himself or herself and seek employment in a lower cell at a lower wage rate. Government interference in the natural working of the labour market through protection in any form is warranted only if the reduction in social costs attributable to international phenomena can be substantially reduced.

The vita theory can be used to identify the mechanism underlying one important cause of domestic inefficiency in an industry. A wage premium can be gained by workers in an industry because of a positive M in equation (4.2), but for a positive M to make itself effective the industry must have some ability to vary the price of the end product, p, by passing on any increase in costs to the customer, or to reduce the effects of such a wage premium on its cost by adopting substitute labour-saving capital equipment. A wage premium is frequently associated with restricted entry into the cell over time relative to the demand for labour that would have existed in the absence of the monopoly power of the union. If the workers have financial obligations undertaken at the old, pre-disturbance wage rate, they will fiercely resist any attempt to reduce nominal wages because of the effect of such a real reduction on the burden of their personal debt (Davidson, 1972).

Successful adjustment requires that in response to a change in the mix of output demanded, workers who are displaced from one industry find employment in another. The avoidable social costs are unnecessarily long periods of unemployment. For adjustment to take place with minimal social costs, workers need to have information of job vacancies in other cells and the confidence to undertake the relocation (spatial and temporal) required. They may also need financial assistance in the process of relocation. Anything which can facilitate the reduction of uncertainty about the possibility of beneficial relocation, or can assist in the financing of relocation, must constitute a positive policy (in terms of the OECD's distinction). It is clearly important that any industrial policies designed to slow the needed rate of adjustment must not create uncertainty in the minds of displaced workers so that they delay undertaking relocation in the mistaken hope that the old jobs will re-emerge.

II   LABOUR MARKET CONGESTION

The argument in favour of slowing the rate of adjustment inflicted upon an economy by an international disturbance is that the social costs of adjustment are an *increasing* function of both the magnitude and the severity of the disturbance. In this section social costs are defined in terms of total unemployment caused by a disturbance, and are measured in person-days combining both the number and duration of unemployment. Intervention by government (through some set of commercial policies) may be warranted if the total social costs of adjustment to a specified (series of) disturbance(s) can be substantially reduced. The crucial factor is the speed with which workers, displaced by changes in international conditions, can be dispersed into jobs in other industries, sectors and regions of the economy by the natural mechanisms of the marketplace. The efficiency of the market system can be enhanced by positive policies. Congestion exists when the speed of dispersal is hampered by the post-disturbance pattern of unemployment in terms of a concentration of the unemployed in certain regions, or by certain skills, as well as by the number of unemployed. There is always a case to made for the existence of policies which contribute to the ability of the marketplace to adapt to new conditions, but these measures might need to be strengthened in time of serious change.

The effect of a disturbance in international conditions is to increase the demand for some of the economy's industries, and to reduce demand in others.[2] If the two sets of goods, those with increased or reduced demand, have different production functions in the short run, there will be changes in the derived demand for labour *in terms of its mix.* Some kinds of workers will be unemployed and other categories will be in short supply. The market will clear itself as firms, those directly as well as indirectly affected by the disturbance, respond to change in the relative wage-rates (prices) of different categories of labour, and substitute the cheaper for the dearer to the extent that their existing equipment allows. In the long run, decisions about new capital equipment may take the changes in relative wage-rates into account in determining its labour-intensity. To the extent that changes in relative wage-rates are reflected in the costs of final goods, changed patterns of demand may reduce the need for adjustment. Similarly changes in the different categories of labour will take place in the long and very long runs as workers acquire new and different skills, or downgrade themselves to lower rows in the ranking of skills. These adjustments take place within a seething, dynamic economy in which some firms and sectors are expanding while others retrench, in which wage-rates and other prices are changing, new technology is becoming embodied in capital equipment that is coming on-stream, and the composition of the work force is also undergoing continuous change as old workers retire and new entrants bring different sets of skills. It is likely, self-evidently, to be difficult to isolate the effects of a single, small disturbance. *Per contra,* large disturbances or trend disturbances which reinforce each other and have large cumulative effects, can both impose upon an economy a rate of adjustment in the mix of output and of the utilisation of labour that will exceed any natural capacity of the market. The economy will succeed in expanding the output and utilisation of workers with skills which are in short supply (through overtime and new divisions of labour) to a greater degree than it will find employment for workers with skills and skill levels thrown into excess supply. To the extent that positive manpower policies for upgrading exist, or that firms afflicted with shortages of workers of requisite skills will upgrade their own workers through in-house training programmes, the adjustment mechanism will work more smoothly.[3] Upgrading will also create vacancies for workers of lower skills to aspire to and to fill.

The more narrowly defined the market for individual kinds of labour, the greater the impact may a given disturbance be expected to have insofar as it changes the mix of jobs available in the economy. The emphasis of the vita theory on labour submarkets determined by skill level, industry- and product-specific skills and geographical location, makes the vita theory particularly appropriate for analysis of the process of adjustment. Relative to a theory of labour markets which concerns itself only with a nationwide market for relatively homogeneous factors of production, the vita theory will enhance the likelihood that the market will become congested. The traditional theory of international trade, with its emphasis on internally-mobile homogeneous factors of production, is not appropriate. The existence of compartmentalised markets with impediments to movements among them approaches reality much more closely, and is therefore a more suitable basis for policy-oriented analysis. But the argument for slowing the rate of adjustment can be validated even in highly simplified models. Leamer (1980) has shown that some diminution in the rate of tariff reduction (and therefore in the rate of displacement out of the declining industry) is inherently desirable in an analysis which assumes that labour is homogeneous, and that all unemployment is voluntary (implying a remarkable adaptability on the part of the physical capital in the expanding industry). Analysis of labour markets in which the degree of mobility is a function of (historical) time is much better suited to a work in which displaced workers are faced with imperfect information, the possible lack of outlets in which to utilise their available skills and with the possible loss of some industry- or product-specific k as well as some wage premium.

The argument for slowing the rate of adjustment to an international disturbance by means of some set of commercial policy measures in the presence of labour market congestion has two roots. First, the fact of congestion increases the total social cost as the unaided market works quite slowly to disperse the displaced workers. Second, the uncertainty created in workers competing for jobs in congested markets is likely to slow decisions to adapt to the new conditions, as well as impeding attempts at upgrading and/or spatial relocation. In other words, congestion may by itself constitute a negative manpower policy.

The theory of congestion can usefully be considered in two sets of circumstances: a broad version which suggests that adaptation is more difficult when the national labour market is suffering from widespread excess supply, and a narrow version which argues that the ability of the market to disperse displaced workers will be affected by the distribution of the unemployment in individual submarkets or cells of the regional matrices. The narrow version is compatible with potential balance in the number of jobs available, and sought at the going average wage-rate: the problem is purely one of mismatches by skill, skill level and location. The broad version implies a deficiency of aggregate demand.

		Regions			
	1	2	3	4	5
Senior executive	0	0	0	0	0
Professional	0	ed	0	0	0
Upper management	0	ed	0	0	0
Middle management	0	0	0	0	ed
Highly-skilled blue-collar	0	0	es	0	ed
Medium-skilled blue-collar	0	es	es	0	ed
Production worker	0	es	es	0	0
Unskilled worker	0	0	0	0	0

FIGURE 4.1 *The net demand matrix of labour markets* *

* Each cell contains a symbol, *ed*, 0 or *es*, which denote respectively excess demand, balance or excess supply in the labour market identified. Positive numbers are associated with *ed* and negative numbers with *es* when actual values are used.

Figure 4.1 presents a schematic version of the excess demand and supply matrix of labour submarkets, and permits an easy distinction to be drawn between the competing hypotheses. The actual figure shows the narrow version of the congestion hypothesis. The matrix is highly simplified since it compresses into a single category all occupations which require the same skill level. This allows a single matrix to show the geographical and skill level dimensions. The hypothesised disturbance has created unemployment in five cells. These five cells show the unemployed to have very similar skill levels, and to be geographically concentrated. The geographical concentration makes the seeking-out of a vacancy at the same skill level more difficult when the vacancies are some distance away, simply because the quality of information may be expected to deteriorate with distance. The corresponding cells with excess demand are shown to be geographically distant, and three cells require higher levels of skill. The narrow version of the congestion hypothesis exists if the ability of the market place to disperse (absorb) the redundant workers (in cells marked *es*) into other occupations is less under the conditions shown, than it would have been had the same number of unemployed been widely scattered throughout the matrix (and the corresponding *ed* cells equally widely scattered). The presumption is that the mix of job vacancies changes, in the normal way of evolution, only slowly so that a concentrated surge of unemployed workers in adjacent cells will be hard for the market to reallocate, and will inevitably require changes in relative wage rates and the adaptation of the stock of capital and the mix of output. The more distant the cells with excess demand (vertically or horizontally), the greater the change in the required profile of the labour force and the more difficult will that be to achieve. When a vacancy occurs at a higher level than that in which the unemployed worker is to be found, it is reasonable to suppose that a series of adjustments will be needed as an individual worker will only have the capacity to aspire to moving up a single row. Similarly, geographical distance is likely to reduce the quality of information so that the probability that a worker in one column will successfully fill a job at the same skill level in another (distant) column is smaller: this process too could require multiple adaptation. There is, therefore, an argument for controlling the rate of adjustment required of an economy in terms of both the magnitude of the disturbance and in terms of its severity. The broad version of the congestion hypothesis can also be visualised in terms of Figure 4.1 by imagining that all the bottom four rows of cells contain an excess supply of labour *prior* to the disturbance. Thus while the disturbance might create as many jobs as it eliminates, the level of aggregate demand is deficient for the national labour market to clear.

Parsons (1980) has examined empirically the desirability of some kind of intervention (or protection) being offered to industries on the basis of labour market congestion. His study supports the existence of the broad, but not the narrow, version of the congestion hypothesis. Since an argument for protection can only be applied to the narrow version, Parsons' study warrants attention.[4] The theoretical framework is set in the highly abstract level of optimal intervention policy in a world characterised by homogeneous labour and competitive markets. Any recognition of industry-specific skills or geographical congestion is implicit, and is recognised only in the fact that regressions are run on two-digit industry-level data.[5] The theoretical model does, however, recognise that reabsorption of displaced workers into the employed labour force may take time because of some straightforward difficulty in any market of matching vacancies and unemployed workers. It is also recognised that the period of unemployment will vary with the intensity of the search effort on the part of the displaced workers.

To his own surprise, Parsons' empirical work on US data shows that the rate at which workers have been displaced from an industry accelerates the rate at which they find employment in other firms or industries. This finding appears to refute the narrow version of the congestion hypothesis. Parsons' empirical model, constrained by the data available, consists of an auto-regressive regression equation:

$$UR = a_0 + a_1 UR_{-1} + a_2(UR_{-1})^2 + a_3 UR_{-1}.URE + a_4 UR_{-1}.RPROB + a_5 L + a_6 R + e \quad (4.3)$$

where UR is the stock of people unemployed in an industry or sector as a percentage of the total work force in that industry or sector. In the absence of the composite variables involving UR_{-1} (the second, third and fourth independent variables), the coefficient a_1 measures the rate of retention in unemployment of job losers. The variables L and R measure the effects of further layoffs or recalls respectively. The composite variables identify factors which effect the retention rate, and therefore the validity of the congestion hypotheses. URE measures aggregate unemployment so that a_3 identifies the broad version of the hypothesis. $RPROB$ measures the probability of recall. The datum used for this measure is the ratio of unemployed job losers on layoff to total unemployed job losers in the industry or sector. This measure is not blessed with good rules of correspondence[6] because it takes no account of the cause of the displacement which might be cyclical (implying a transitory disturbance) or it might be a permanent disturbance, in which even a high ratio of job losers on layoff to total unemployed losers might indicate actual (narrow) congestion of workers laid off from a particular industry. Finally, and of primary concern here, is the variable $(UR_{-1})^2$ which is used to measure the sensitivity of the retention rate to (nonlinear) variation in the rate itself. This is the coefficient used by Parsons to assess the validity of the narrow version. The regressions were run for 'all manufacturing', 'all durable goods manufacturing', 'all non-durable goods manufacturing' and ten two-digit industries.

The coefficient a_3 was positive throughout and statistically significant in eleven regressions. This result clearly supports the broad version of the theory of labour-market congestion: the absorption of displaced workers back into the labour force will take longer the greater the overall unemployment rate. The coefficient a_2 was consistently negative and frequently statistically significant. This is the evidence which is interpreted as rejecting the narrow version of the labour-market congestion hypothesis: reabsorption will take longer and social costs will be higher if displaced workers have the same or very similar skill levels and specific skills, and if they are geographically concentrated. The likelihood of recall measure shows positive coefficients consistently, but is significant only in the more aggregative equations and in the automotive and fabricated metals industries. Both industries could reasonably expect some resurgence in the demand for their products.

The persistently negative values of a_2 should not be taken as conclusive evidence against the narrow version of the congestion hypothesis. Weaknesses in both data and methodology limit the reliance that can be placed on Parsons' interpretation of his results. The features of the model involving perfect competition in labour markets, and homogeneity of labour within a sector or industry, make the test less than fully applicable to the narrow version based on the vita theory. Data availability limits the test to employment rates in industries or sectors rather than by skill levels or in geographical regions. Over the period for which the tests were conducted (January 1968 to January 1976), the overall rate of unemployment was quite low in the earlier years. Annual data (from the US Bureau of Labor Statistics) show the following annual average unemployment rates: 1968, 3.2 per cent (against a full-employment benchmark rate of 4.0 per cent, and with unemployment among white adult males down to 2.0 per cent); 1969, 3.1 per cent; 1970, 4.5; 1971, 5.4; 1972, 5.0; 1973, 4.3; 1974, 5.0; 1975, 7.8 and January 1976, 7.9 per cent. The months for which the unemployment rate increased sharply coincided with the introduction of much less stringent conditions for eligibility for supplementary income under the Trade Adjustment Assistance programme (Aho and Bayard, 1980). The generosity of this programme might well induce laid-off workers to reduce the intensity of their search, and the retention rate might show a trend which was picked up in URE or $(UR_{-1})^2$. If the trend is picked up in the latter variable, the negative values of the coefficient a_2 are even more difficult to explain. All the industries, with the possible exception of clothing/apparel, are likely to be industries in which wage premiums exist.

The most important qualification to Parsons' data and model as vehicles for the study of the narrow version or the congestion hypothesis lies in the very short lag employed. Limiting the observed reaction to a single month suggests that workers can find alternative occupations quite quickly if they decide that recall into 'their' industry is unlikely in the short run. In fact, the one-month lag suggests that a_2 might be a better measure (as an inverse) of the likelihood of recall than a_4. It is possible that the negative values of a_2 show that workers, when unemployment rates in their industries are high, seek alternative occupations more intensely, and that the greater intensity of search is rewarded. Those workers who leave the employment rolls in their sector or industry are likely simply to have downgraded themselves into temporary occupations in local markets (and to have bumped other unemployed in the process). Workers who take temporary, lower-skilled positions may still have expectations that they will be recalled into their industry when its fortunes improve. According to this interpretation, the reduction in the sector's or industry's unemployment rate does not indicate that workers have been reabsorbed into the labour force at a skill level with which they would be satisfied on other than a temporary, makeshift basis. The time horizon of one month is simply too short for the results to be taken as a refutation of the narrow version of the congestion hypothesis.

If the *rate* of adjustment imposed upon an economy by international disturbances is to serve as a possible argument for protection, that is, for slowing the rate of adjustment, then the narrow version of the congestion hypothesis is important. When the disturbance which causes short-run structural unemployment has its origin in the international sector, it is likely that adjacent cells in the matrix of labour markets will experience similar effects. When industries lose their international competitiveness as comparative advantage shifts among nations, the industries which are subjected to severe competition are likely to employ similar mixes of factors of production. Consider a change in comparative advantage caused by evolution over time so that industries which use low-skilled labour intensively lose their international competitiveness, and all industries which have similar mixes of factors of production (similar degrees of reliance upon low-skilled workers) will become vulnerable to foreign competition within a short period. The workers displaced by import competition will tend to resemble each other in skill levels if not in industry-specific or product-specific skill. The greater the elasticity of supply of the affected industries, the greater is the magnitude of the disturbance likely to be. Such conditions do prevail with the sudden development of manufacturing capacity in the newly-industrialising areas. The industries which have been adversely affected are those with similar input mixes: predominantly heavy reliance upon production workers in which the older, developed world has a substantial per–unit cost disadvantage. International disturbances are likely, then, to bring about instances in which the narrow version might be expected to apply.

The logical argument in favour of the narrow version of the congestion hypothesis is very strong. Given the weakness of the test applied by Parsons, the narrow version should be accepted in the absence of further evidence. The costs of sudden adjustment leading to prolonged and geographically–concentrated bouts of unemployment are magnified by any multiplier effects on the local regional economy, and in the context of the US, at least by the possibility of some disruption of financial markets and government services if local political entities default on their debt.

The broad version of the congestion hypothesis, while not acceptable as an argument for increasing barriers to international trade because of the likelihood of retaliation by trading partners, does have policy relevance in terms of scheduled reductions of commercial barriers. Since the Second World War, the industrial world has made great strides in reducing the height of barriers to trade through multilateral negotiations under the auspices of the GATT. Recognising the need for gradualness, the reductions in trade barriers have been scheduled to be phased in over a period of years. The broad version would argue for a delay in the introduction of scheduled reductions during a recession. Clearly quite specific conditions and definitions would need to be worked out in advance, but the notion has significant common-sense appeal. The most difficult problem to be resolved would be whether all nations should interrupt their planned schedules for the reduction of tariffs and other barriers, or only those in recession. The scheme might gain political acceptance most easily if it were couched in terms of a general postponement in terms of a recession in the OECD rather than in any single nation. This would allow the industrial nations to bend their efforts on the collective reduction of their common recession, and to reintroduce the agreed-to reduction in trade barriers when prosperity has been regained.

III SENILE INDUSTRY PROTECTION

A *senile industry* is defined as one which has lost its comparative cost advantage (or whose comparative disadvantage has grown to exceed transportation costs). The cause of such a loss of comparative advantage could come quite suddenly as necessary technology becomes available in countries which had been unable to compete in the good in question, or when a liaison is established between a cost-efficient producer in one country and an established marketing-and-distribution system in the potential importer. The latter case will apply only to so-called experience goods, which are most likely to require a sophisticated marketing-and-distribution organisation (involving after-sales service and warranty support) in an industrial or developed nation. A second cause of such a loss of comparative advantage could be the natural evolution of economies over time, and particularly the emergence of industrial capacity in countries with ample supplies of labour at low cost (cf. Akamatsu, 1962). Both causes could merge and give rise to a natural increase in competitiveness of erstwhile developing countries which have been transformed into newly-industrialised countries or areas. In this, the transfer of technology under the *aegis* of the multinational corporation will be important. A senile industry must be distinguished from an 'injured industry' which is usually seen as having lost its comparative cost advantage or ability to compete successfully with imports because of negotiated reductions in the level of protection. Because a senile industry is one that is no longer able to compete in its market without government support, there is no question about its being allowed to continue to exist indefinitely. The question is 'What rate of phase-out is best?' Should the industry be allowed to contract at the rate dictated by unalloyed market forces, or is there some rationale for intervention on the part of the authorities to slow, but not stop, the rate of contraction?

The essence of a senile industry lies in the existence of industry-specific inputs. If industry-specific inputs exist, particularly in human and physical capital, the sudden demise of the industry will rescue the capital stock of the importing national. Workers with industry-specific human capital will always have some general human capital as well, and are therefore reemployable at lower wage-rates in other industries. Physical capital may not have an alternative use. The purpose of senile industry protection would be to avoid an unnecessarily large reduction in the capital stock of the nation. The two questions are: should the industry be protected, and if so, what protective mechanism is the most suitable? In Gray (1973), the argument was made for a quota as the most effective commercial policy tool, but Wood (1975) successfully argued the case for a subsidy.

In Hillman (1982), the argument for senile-industry protection is seen as an argument made on the basis of 'social justice': the intent behind slowing the speed of adjustment is ostensibly to preserve the level of income of the owners of industry-specific factors of production. Such an argument is essentially subjective, and was only indirectly related to the original reason suggested for senile industry protection, which is strictly one of maintaining the capital stock. Of course there is clearly an overlap between the two arguments since protecting a senile industry necessarily does tend to maintain the incomes of the owners of the specific capital and prevents them from dissaving. In an earlier piece, Hillman (1977) applies the whole panoply of neoclassical assumptions reported in Chapter 2 (including static analysis) to question the desirability of senile industry protection. Then in a brief excursion into the adjustment process (1977, p. 158) he casually assumes away the whole problem by allowing the industry-specific capital to continue to be used in the senile industry so that it is fully depreciated, and is then transferred into another industry or consumer according to the dictates of consumers' intertemporal allocation decisions.

Industry-specific and product-specific capital can both lose value if the surge of imports displaces domestic production at a speed in excess of the rate of depreciation of physical capital equipment, and the rate of retirement of workers in whom the specific human capital is embodied. The physical capital will have its value reduced to salvage value (unless sold to the new exporters). The following argument is presented in terms of human capital, which is the more complex rationale for intervention. In practice, the loss of human capital would be added to any loss of net present value of the physical capital involved.[7]

When the job of an experienced worker with some product- or industry-specific human capital is destroyed by import competition, the cost to society and to the individual is the difference between the present value of the worker's human capital in the alternative (next-best) employment and the present value of the human capital that would be achieved with a specified package of protection in the affected (senile) industry. The return in the alternative employment must be measured net of any costs of retraining, and the return from protection must be measured net of any loss of gains from trade. If the senile industry is domestically efficient and no wage premium exists, then the cost to the worker and to society are equal, except for the loss to society of any gain from trade. Any transfer payment from society to the worker merely involves the question of whether the worker bears the whole cost. If the industry is not domestically efficient, the worker's cost will exceed the social cost.

Product-specific human capital is attributable to both training and experience. The present value of employment in an alternative occupation will be reduced by any costs of retraining, by any time spent unemployed and by an inability of the displaced worker to achieve the senile industry rate of return on *general* human capital. The greater the loss of current (national) income due to the displacement, and the greater the costs of adjustment to the alternative employment, the stronger is the argument for phase-out protection. The larger the net loss, the more gradual should the phase-out be. However, this is not a matter subject to precise computation, and the determination of the appropriate package calls for nice judgment on the part of the authorities. The argument for the imposition of senile industry protection loses strength as faith in the quality of the judgment of the authority declines.

Using K_i to represent the capitalised value of returns to human capital in different industries (k_i), the criteria for senile industry protection and for retraining can be expressed quite simply:

criterion for protection $$K_j - C > K_g \qquad (4.4)$$

criterion for retraining $$K_a - R > K_g \qquad (4.5)$$

where K_j is the present value of the human capital in industry j (both general and specific) of those displaced and C is the present cost of protection however imposed.[8] Both are computed for protection of a specified amount for a specified time. K_g is the capitalised value of the general (transferable) human capital of those displaced. K_a is the capitalised value of the human capital of retrained workers in the alternative industry, a, and R is the present cost of retraining. Both criteria require that the present value of human capital in the senile or the alternative industry exceed the return to the general human capital of those displaced from the senile industry. The smaller is K_g – the greater the length of time for which displaced workers remain unemployed and the greater the drop in their social product – the stronger is the argument for protection and/or for retraining. The protection and retraining criteria are not mutually exclusive. In view of the international repercussions of protecting a senile industry (even though such protection could be considered to be authorised by Clause XIX of the GATT), there is a strong case for retraining if the two criteria are of something like equal magnitude.[9]

The factors affecting K_j are important for an understanding of the strength of the case for senile industry protection. The excess of K_j over K_g depends in part upon the amount of industry-specific human capital of workers in the senile industry (K_j). This quantity will vary with the age and experience of the workers likely to be displaced. Experience is positively related with specific human capital and additional formal training may be acquired during the years employed in the industry (although the value of formal training will increase less quickly with the experience and age of the worker). Young workers' industry-specific capital will be smaller because of less experience. The costs of retraining and of obtaining alternative employment (the intervening period of unemployment) are also likely to be positively related to age and experience. Older workers may have become less adaptable so that the costs of retraining per unit of human capital generated may also be expected to increase with age. This factor is likely to make older workers more willing to downgrade themselves and to seek employment in markets with requirements of human capital lower than their own capital, but also lower than their own general human capital. Older industries (with older work forces) are more likely to warrant senile industry protection.

To the extent that workers who are displaced are preponderantly older workers within striking distance of normal retirement age, the social justice aspects of the question might be solved by giving early retirement bonuses. Such an approach does not avoid the diminution of capital, but it might be preferable to the erection of barriers to international trade in marginal cases.

IV   REINFORCING DISTURBANCES

To this point the chapter has assumed that the sole source of required adjustment was to be found in a change in international conditions. Changes in international trading conditions can be reinforced or diminished by the lingering effects of past disturbances which have not been fully adjusted to or by the immediate effects of concomitant disturbances of domestic origin. The question of adjustment must be seen as a reaction to a composite change in underlying conditions (including political phenomena) rather than as the consequence of a single identifiable event. The composite disturbance will include not only the effects of past disturbances which linger on, but also the effects of a release from a suppressed disequilibrium caused by an earlier unwillingness to bear the social costs inherent in adjustment.

The recent years have been plentifully supplied with disturbances of substantial magnitude. These range from the US inflation induced by the Vietnamese war; the release in 1973 of the overvaluation of the US dollar during the waning years of the Bretton Woods era; the 1974 and 1979 oil price shocks; the severe global recession induced by the tight money policies of the UK and the US and the spectacular achievements in their export markets of the East Asian economies, including both Japan and the 'four little dragons' (Hong Kong, Korea, Singapore and Taiwan). In the eighties, these disturbances will continue to require adjustments but will be joined by such new developments as the reentry of the People's Republic of China into the world economy, and by the new technological revolution through which the world must pass and to which it must adapt: Meade (1983) aptly describes this combination of innovations in communications, information services, control systems and production automation as 'Chips and Robots'. Finally there is the possibility of a new wave of foreign direct investment by multinational corporations (MNCs) bent on serving home markets (in industrialised countries) with production from Third World nations. While none of these disturbances can be considered to be purely domestic, each of them represents a disturbance which will reinforce the type of adjustment required by developed nations, which is to adapt to new competition from cheap labour countries.

The formal question of whether a domestic disturbance is reinforcing or partially offsetting a disturbance which is already having its effect, can be considered in terms of Figure 4.1. Two disturbances are self-reinforcing if:

(a) the numbers of displaced people in the excess-supply cells increase as a result of the inclusion of the second disturbance.
(b) the distance between cells with excess supply and those with excess demand increases.
(c) the total number of jobs is reduced more by the combination of disturbances.

(d) the cells with excess supply are more closely concentrated enhancing the narrow theory of factor-market congestion.

The Chips-and-Robots revolution would seem to present significant difficulties of adaptation for developed economies without any aggravation from international markets. Chips and Robots are likely to displaced lower-skilled workers first, and it is these very workers (and the labour-intensive industries in which they are employed) who are vulnerable to existing foreign trade stresses. The use of industrial policies has been designed almost exclusively to maintain industries in which the industrial countries no longer have a comparative cost advantage. Reliance by MNCs upon foreign sources of supply, particularly in countries where they are encouraged to locate subsidiaries equipped with new up-to-date technology by the establishment of export zones with all the inducements that such zones offer, will further aggravate the problem of finding gainful employment for displaced production workers.

In a graph with social costs measured on the vertical axis, and the required rate of adjustment on the horizontal axis, a function would be shown as a curve rising and becoming quite steep. The existence of a second, reinforcing disturbance shifts the function upwards and, if anything, enhances its upward slope. Neglect of such a relationship is inevitable in analyses set in comparative static, general equilibrium. Even when economic growth is explicitly countenanced, the potential for dislocation and adjustment seems to be deemphasised as in Krueger (1980, p. 225): 'Moreover, because structural adjustment in the developed countries is in any event necessary for economic growth, it can be cogently argued that competition from LDC imports will, in fact, speed up the growth process.' There is the implicit assumption of a pull disturbance, while in reality the industrial world is beset by push phenomena.

Despite the cogency of the argument that changes in international conditions can give grounds for slowing the rate of adjustment in order to reduce the social costs, the formation and implementation of policy is no easy matter. Disturbances frequently do not allow themselves to be easily diagnosed. Threatened industries are visible but the decision to implement protection and to allow that protection to wane as the economy adapts requires political determination that is sometimes rare in a democracy (but see Hillman, 1982). The phenomenon of accelerated adjustment may be quickly identified, but the distinction between a senile industry and an industry which is only at a temporary disadvantage is not easily drawn. Factor-market congestion may be difficult to distinguish from simple recessionary tendencies.

The generally accepted method of supporting an industry in order to reduce the rate of change which conditions are imposing on it is by means of a subsidy. This method has the additional advantage that, where strings are attached to the protection, as in Curzon Price's concept of industrial policies or in granting conditional protection (outlined in Chapter 3), firms which choose not to accede to the conditions can easily be excluded from the protection and can be left to fend for themselves. The problem with any programme involving a subsidy lies in the means by which the needed funds are raised and the opportunity costs of those funds.

In the rough and tumble of modern politics, so-called voluntary export restraints and similar measures are likely to be preferred. These may serve the purpose of reducing the rate of increase of imports, but the Multifibre Arrangement in textiles and clothing or apparel, for all its lip-service to phasing out protection, seems to have turned into a system of permanent protection of the existing capacity.

5 The Possibility of Permanent Unemployment

Building on Smith and Mill, modern analyses of international trade and of the gains which are to be derived from the unimpeded exchange of goods and services incorporate the assumption that resources in all countries are fully utilised. Meade's modern classic (1955) is no exception. The doctrine of free trade must, therefore, accept the same presumption: that full employment will exist under conditions of perfectly free trade (given adequate aggregate demand). In terms of the definitions of adjustment given in Chapter 1, a lack of compatibility of free trade with full employment would constitute a case of 'chronic' adjustment costs. Under such conditions, workers displaced from import-competing industries would not be able to find alternative employment at a welfare subsistence income.[1] As noted, 'chronic' in this context must mean that unemployment and adjustment costs endure for longer than is socially tolerable. The allegation that adjustment costs are 'chronic' does not require proof that a freely operating system of global markets would not be able to achieve full employment in some far, far distant time.

However, there is a danger that in seeking such a proof, the analyst would require recourse to variables which economic analysis normally eschews – in particular the introduction of population growth rates as endogenous variables. Consider the possible argument that the net reproduction rate of families was positively related to income for families with less than the median income so that unemployed workers would tend to have low net reproduction rates (presumably in response to inadequate health delivery systems in poor neighbourhoods and the high cost of health care). Given excess population in the world in which labour surpluses exist in poor countries, and 'chronic unemployment' prevails in industrialised countries, a long-run market-induced equilibrium in the global labour

70

market might entail negative net reproduction rates for low-income families. Traditional economic analysis usually makes the implicit assumption that the political system is not disrupted during the period required to reach a new equilibrium and that society does not lapse in anarchy under the burden of widespread and enduring poverty and, into this context, negative net reproduction rates (high infant mortality rates) in poor families. Putting the issue of political stability aside as transcending the scope of formal economic analysis, it would be possible to build a model showing that free trade and full employment must ultimately be reconcilable (and that chronic unemployment is impossible). The length of time required for the adjustment of world population could well involve certain generations of individuals being unemployed for their whole lifetimes. The issue of political stability could not, under such conditions, be realistically put aside without some recognition of the need for fundamental changes in the operation of the societies involved. The problem would push beyond the boundaries of formal analysis inherent in the free-trade doctrines: modern welfare analyses with their narrow criteria of efficiency would simply not be applicable.

Chronic adjustment costs will be experienced when there exists an absolute shortage of jobs in a country when labour is priced at subsistence income. Such a possibility can be considered when labour is treated as a homogeneous factor of production, and changes in international trading conditions destroy more jobs than they create. This is the concern of Section I. The more interesting and more probable condition for the existence of chronic adjustment costs involves heterogeneous labour and an enduring mismatch between the skill-mix of labour supplied by the working population and that demanded by the productive sector. Section II examines the limits of the ability of an industrialised economy to adapt to a surge of imports that displaces workers with low skills and to generate demand for exports which utilise high-skilled workers more intensively. This condition reflects a sudden increase in export capacity on the part of the newly-industrialising areas and their successor industrialising countries (Lorenz, 1983). The question here is whether the unskilled workers in the industrial countries will be able to achieve gainful employment at a welfare-subsistence wage. The essence of the problem is a change in the mix of labour demanded rather than a change in the number of jobs. Section II must also consider the likelihood that Chips and Robots will accentuate the strains caused in the labour markets in industrialised nations by the growth of export capacity of the newly-industrialising exporters. In practice, it is quite possible that new conditions in international trade and technological innovations will reduce the total demand for labour *and* will alter the mix of skills demanded. Finally, Section III considers the possibility that a discrepancy will exist between the money wage compatible with welfare-subsistence in the North and the South because of unequal standards, different historical experiences and the unequal cost (in a world numeraire) of domestic (non-tradable) goods.

I   PERMANENT UNEMPLOYMENT WITH HOMOGENEOUS
    LABOUR

The problem of permanent unemployment in rich (industrial) nations has been adumbrated by one of the fundamental theorems of the Heckscher–Ohlin–Samuelson model of international trade. The theorem states that unimpeded free trade will, under certain specific and very constraining assumptions, generate absolute factor-price equalisation in both (all) countries. The assumptions are so recherché as to make the theorem non-operational (see Caves, 1960, p. 77). Heckscher's original version of the factor-proportions theory showed a tendency toward factor-price equalisation under the assumption of universal full employment (Caves, 1960, p. 25). Advocates of free trade have always managed to divorce the implications of the factor-proportions theorem for the integration of the world labour markets (as is implicit in factor-price equalisation tendencies) from the existence of substantial and apparently intractable labour surpluses in the developing and underdeveloped countries of the world. The full-employment assumption is suspect. The inconsistency between the assumption of full employment and the reality of labour surpluses in the Third World (and high population growth rates) may be identified as one of the sources of strain in the North–South dialogue when northern protestations and rhetoric sit uneasily with their pragmatic negotiating stance. This gap between rhetoric and fact is particularly apparent in negotiations on international trade in textiles and clothing (apparel; see Chapter 6). Unimpeded international trade integrates labour markets in the same industry in two competing nations. In a world of integrated national labour markets, international trade integrates the global labour market subject to the effects of man-made and natural impediments (such as tariffs and transportation costs respectively). There is an important *caveat* in that the discipline imposed on labour by unrestrained international competition will be much less direct, and therefore less powerful on industries not involved in international trade. It is possible, then, that wage premiums in non-tradable-goods industries could continue to exist for protracted periods if only the slightest imperfection in labour markets were granted. Within the confines of the factor-proportions theory, perfectly free trade between the industrialised North and labour-surplus countries in Africa, Asia and Latin America will reduce wages or employment in the industrialised countries and effect some partial equalisation of the rate of surplus labour. While there would be a corresponding increase in world income and world demand, the additional demand in erstwhile labour-surplus countries will be divided between the demand for high-technology and capital-intensive imports and domestic goods. The redistribution of world income combined with the greater affluence of the poor nations may, in the long run, validate Say's Law, but in the interim, there could be widespread unemployment in industrialised nations.[2]

Traditional economic theory assumes that the capital stock (with its embodied technology) is sufficient to employ the available labour force at a better-than-subsistence wage. Unemployment is considered either to be frictional or is considered a cyclical matter, except in developing countries in which the possibility of surplus labour is countenanced. There the Malthusian result is usually assumed to be avoided by the social network and the phenomenon of underemployment. The interrelationships which underlie the assumption of full employment in industrialised countries can be examined in terms of Figure 5.1, which shows an aggregate production function for a nation in autarchy. Labour (L) can be substituted for capital (K) between the two ridge lines (R_K and R_L), which join points on isoquants showing varying levels of output of a composite good at which the marginal products of the inputs is zero. The only isoquant drawn is that which fully employs the existing stock of capital (K) and the existing stock of labour (L) and it shows other combinations of capital and labour which will yield the same output. Because labour requires some minimum income to survive and to maintain its energy level, the actual range of substitutability of capital and labour is less than that shown by the two ridge lines: the dotted line (I_L) is drawn as an isocline with slope WW which denotes the wage rate compatible with welfare subsistence income (for a description of ridge lines and isoclines, see Ferguson, 1969, pp. 161-73).[3] Full employment of the stock of labour (L) is possible at welfare subsistence income or better if S_L intersects I_F to the left of the isocline with tangent WW. This apparently simple diagram has some extremely subtle assumptions built into it. By focusing on production of a composite good, the diagram does not allow for changes in the mix of goods demanded and supplied.[4] Changes in income distribution and tastes will affect the mix of output and therefore the relative returns to factors at full employment: the isoquant is a series of general equilibrium solutions rather than the familiar concept of microeconomics which assumes a constancy of output of a single good throughout its length. When the country begins to engage in international trade or, more in context, when the capacity of foreign nations to supply labour–intensive imports increases substantially over a short period of time, the mix of output changes, a new composite commodity evolves and the position and shape of I_F change. Increased supplies of labour-intensive goods from abroad reduce the demand for labour relative to that of capital (used intensively in the concomitant exports). The result of such a change is to shift I_F to the left and with it, R_K, I_L and R_L. Chronic unemployment may be created by a change in the conditions prevailing in international markets. In terms of a simple supply-and-demand for labour diagram, Figure 5.2 shows the change in international trading patterns shifting the demand for

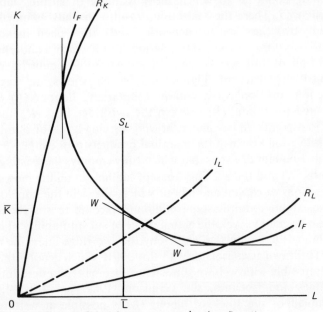

FIGURE 5.1   *Aggregate production function*

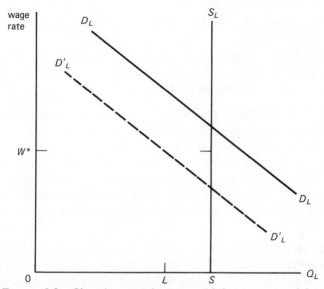

FIGURE 5.2 *Chronic unemployment with homogeneous labour*
The shift in labour demand follows from the change in the mix of goods
demanded. The wage rate, W^*, is compatible with welfare subsistence
income and LS units of labour are shown as chronically unemployed.

labour to the left, clearing the market at less than subsistence income.

Figure 5.1 is a complex diagram since the change in the shape and
position of I_F must take into account not only the direct change in the
pattern of international trade but also the induced effects of a
different distribution of income as well as any increase in national real
income due to the favourable shift in the net barter terms of trade. If
some labour-intensive goods have demand which is highly income-
elastic for capitalists and these goods are protected from foreign
competition by exorbitant transportation costs (they are non-
tradables), then the shift in I_F will be smaller and the likelihood of
chronic unemployment is reduced. Figure 5.1 also assumes a given
technology to be embodied in the physical capital and in the
production functions for the individual components of the composite
good. If that technology suddenly changes and is replaced by a
technology with major labour-saving characteristics, the likelihood of
chronic unemployment is enhanced. The increase in export capacity of
the newly-industrialising countries and the new Chips-and-Robots
revolution reinforce each other. The situation can be even further
aggravated by the synergy between the two since MNCs will now be
able to transfer to developing nations the labour-saving technology

which will magnify the capacity of those countries to provide cheap manufactured goods to the industrialised world.

The possibility of chronic unemployment affecting generations of workers and the implication of such a shock for the stability of the political system is touched on by Nordheimer (1983):

> After three decades of prosperity, unemployment among the nine member nations of the Common Market has exceeded 11 per cent, affecting a total of 12.3 million people and the number is climbing. Forty-two per cent of this total belongs to the under-25 age group, and this figure does not include the hundreds of thousands of 16- to 18-year olds who are in some form of government subsidised training. Nor does it include even larger groups in schools or universities.

The same report quotes a career counsellor in Britain as warning that 'unless the economy can be restructured to find work again for the less skilled, it will be a recipe for disaster'. Nordheimer also reports that in the Netherlands a university-sponsored survey of 16- and 17-year olds found widespread antagonism of a right-wing mentality directed against foreign workers, and a surprising 8 per cent arguing for the establishment of 'national purity' as a political goal. These sentiments exist despite what are, historically, relatively generous social welfare systems. While evidence of this sort is almost inevitably disjointed and falls short of the hard criteria of econometric practice, it cannot simply be disregarded because either no sponsor has been found to conduct a scientific survey of major breadth and depth, or because the attitudes do not lend themselves to quantification. Hindley and Nicolaides (1983, p. 50) point out that if the cost of subsidising unemployment exceeds the cost of transfer payments paid to the unemployed, the rest of the country is better off *from an economic point of view* by tolerating the unemployment. While their statement is perfectly correct, it recalls the myopia of the Krauss model (see Chapter 2). Economics is not conducted in a vacuum and economic analysis, which is ostensibly policy-oriented, must take the realities of political variables into account.

Failure to take cyclical factors into account reinforces the narrowness of analyses that assume full employment (or maximal employment). What may be socially tolerable in a period of high global demand for goods may prove intolerable when the countries which are experiencing chronic labour surplus for the first time in years are also wallowing in the depths of a recession.

II PERMANENT UNEMPLOYMENT WITH HETEROGENEOUS LABOUR

Once the possibility of distinguishing among workers is introduced into the analytic framework, it becomes feasible for the labour market to be characterised by mismatches of the mix of skills demanded and supplied. This section is concerned with the effect on employment in the industrialised world of a push disturbance involving increased capacity for exports from newly-industrialising and developing nations. The presumption is that these nations will sell more goods using low-skilled labour relatively intensively and will import, in exchange, goods using much capital, high technology and highly skilled labour. This disturbs the economy of the industrial importer by adding to the demand for highly-skilled labour and detracting from the demand for low-skilled labour.

A structural excess of supply of low-skilled workers will exist formally when the existing patterns of demand for production of goods and services in the industrialised nation has a derived demand for labour that fully utilises the available supply of (many kinds of) highly-skilled workers before the supply of low-skilled workers approaches exhaustion. Attempts to cure structural unemployment of this kind by means of aggregate demand policies will be frustrated by bottlenecks in the production of goods which use highly-skilled workers intensively. The physical capital stock and the embodied technology are assumed constant in the short run. The structural unemployment becomes chronic when, in the very long run, the mismatch between skills demanded and supplied continues to exist even though the wage of workers competing in the markets (the row in the matrix) for unskilled labour has reached welfare subsistence income. In the present time, the possibility of chronic structural unemployment of low-skilled workers seems likely to affect the industrialised countries before the problem of chronic unemployment of (homogeneous) labour in the sense that the society cannot create enough employment opportunities at subsistence income. Chronic unemployment of low-skilled workers is the problem created by the surge in the capacity for exports of manufactured goods by the newly-industrialising nations. It may be that the problem of skill-mix is merely an earlier stage of a chronic total excess supply of labour to be endured when the full impact of the new labour-saving technology is experienced.

There is a 'natural tendency' for those people who remain

unemployed for any length of time to be those with the lowest skills. The process of bumping involves the downgrading of the level of the market in which a worker seeks employment: the process is undertaken by the worker at his/her own volition when the cost of upgrading through training up to a new level of skill is seen not to warrant the expected return on the training, and when no employment at the original skill level is available. The displaced worker will seek employment in a market in which the owned stock of (general) human capital provides a competitive edge. This downgrading will displace another worker who will in turn bump a third worker in an even lower market. Given the prevalence and logical self-interest of bumping, it follows that the greater part of people who remain unemployed for protracted periods will tend to be those with low levels of skill.

The heterogeneity of the labour force, which is the focus of this section, is the heterogeneity of actual and potential skill levels supplied and demanded. For clarity of exposition, it is useful to refer back to the supply and demand matrices which underlie the net labour demand matrix shown in Figure 4.1. A supply matrix shows the characteristics of the (regional) labour force at a moment in time. The distribution of the numbers in each row, indicating skill levels, may be described as a 'profile'. There exists an equivalent profile for the demand matrix. An incompatibility of the two profiles implies (short-run) structural unemployment. If the demand profile is higher than the supply profile, it is possible that some workers will seek to increase their skills and others will bump workers at lower levels. This is the normal process of adjustment. Relative wages will change leading to greater inducements for workers to upgrade themselves, and leading businesses to substitute labour for capital where feasible. Any apparently chronic unemployment will be seen predominantly in the lower rows of the matrices. Define a category of low-skilled workers as comprising those people whose highest level of attainment entitles them to compete in the lowest three rows of the matrix. Such a category will include unskilled workers and workers with low skill levels: the concept can be made operational by conceiving of low-skilled workers as those whose skills would, in the absence of wage-premium in their particular industry, limit them to a wage-rate of twice the minimum wage-rate. In general terms, low–skilled workers can be thought of as unskilled and semi–skilled workers used mainly in repetitive occupations. That such workers have the potential for chronic excess supply is considered by Cain (1976). Johnson (1978) estimates that the rate of unemployment of unskilled workers in the

US is between 12 and 20 per cent (depending on how skill is defined) even when the aggregate rate of unemployment is about 5 per cent. Since the time when these two authors were writing, the problem is likely to have become more rather than less severe.

The cause of unemployment of low-skilled workers finds its roots in both the demand and supply side of the market. Demand effects derive from changes in the mix of goods demanded, as a result of changes in tastes and foreign supply capabilities, as well as from changes in production functions responding to new technology. Supply-side effects stem from the change in skill endowments of the labour force. In terms of Figure 4.1, demand factors can be attributed to the change in the capacity of the Third World to supply sophisticated manufactured goods and the skill-intensity of their demand for imports, as well as from the rapid movement of industries in the US away from the northern plains to the south–east and the south. Labour-saving technologies would have similar effects. Supply-side effects will evolve much more slowly. These pose a problem when the profile is resistant to upward movement because increasing numbers of workers are locked into their actual level of achievement by virtue of age, low birth vitae or the lack of aspiration. The profile can move downward as industries which suffer decreases in demand are those populated by older workers, and these workers bump lower workers rather than seek to upgrade themselves and as groups with little orientation toward skill-acquisition have higher net reproduction rates.

A mismatch between the two profiles with the demand profile higher than the supply profile (indicating an excess demand for skilled workers and an excess supply of low-skilled workers) can be corrected in the very long run by upgrading workers and by downgrading jobs. Training programmes sought out by the workers themselves, or provided by business or government, can allow workers to increase their skill levels. The process will involve multi-level 'reverse bumping' as each worker strives to move up a single row, and to fill an existing gap or one created by the 'elevation' of a worker from that row. If the demand side changes create as many high-skilled jobs as they displace low-skilled workers, the problem of structual unemployment by skill level would seem to be soluble merely by upgrading the required number of workers. This solution may have been available in the past, but there is a serious question as to whether it is still true in the face of actual and potential shocks which will afflict and are afflicting the industrialised nations over the last quarter of this century.[5]

Structural unemployment of this kind can qualify as 'chronic' if the time required to achieve the elimination of the mismatch is such that individual workers can experience unemployment over the greater part of their potentially productive years. The more demanding the upgrading required, the more likely is the situation to warrant the definition 'chronic'. Inescapably chronic unemployment exists when the demand profile exceeds both the actual supply profile and the *maximum-attainable* supply profile. This possibility countenances limits on the part of people to acquire human capital. The maximum attainable supply profile will vary according to the time dimension. Because workers are born and die, the maximum attainable supply profile is not fixed rigidly thorough time. In the short run, the maximum attainable supply profile is limited by the composition of the work force as it exists, and by the characteristics of those scheduled to enter the work force within the very near future (whose premature vitae can also be considered to be effectively determined). The constraints imposed by the birth vitae and the premature vitae (including formal education and established attitudes towards skill acquisition) are in place. The short-run availability of facilities for upgrading is also a given. In the medium run, governments can introduce changes in the facilities available for upgrading – what are called in Gray (1984) adjustment-facilitating measures: the quality of state-supported programmes can be enhanced, and businesses can be induced (perhaps by tax incentives) to create their own in-house training facilities so that the cost of upgrading is reduced. At the same time, higher returns to skilled workers will increase the perceived benefits of upgrading. Special funding for support might be allocated to workers engaged in upgrading programmes.[6] Finally, in the very long run, governments may be able to increase the efficiency of the formal, state-funded school systems so that all people are equipped to achieve the potential skill level which their genetic endowments permit. This would be the absolute maximum attainable profile constrained by genetic endowments: the supply profile is subject to an absolute constraint. If the demand profile exceeds the absolute maximum attainable supply profile, then structural unemployment is chronic in any sense of that term. Whether or not the maximum attainable supply profile is achieved depends upon the efficiency of the government in the provision of intangible public goods. In practice, the constraint may be significantly more severe than that imposed by genetic endowments.

The increase in the capacity of newly industrialising nations and areas to increase exports to the industrial bloc will lead to a demand for goods using capital, technology and highly-skilled workers. This expectation conforms to the dictates of traditional trade theory. The role of MNCs warrants explicit consideration here because the multinationals are likely to contribute to the evolution of new trade patterns in an important way. In the absence of MNCs, Third World countries' ability to improve the sophistication of their manufactured exports would increase less rapidly as technological knowhow would move more slowly from the industrial bloc to Third World countries. Further, there would tend to be a limit to the degree to which the Third World nations would be able to raise the quality of their product, and by extension, a limit to the volume of manufactured goods which they would be able to supply. This limit would be imposed when the market for standardised manufactures in the industrial bloc was dominantly supplied by exports from the South. But MNCs permit southern economies to produce and to export an additional genus of goods which require a marketing and distribution network within the industrialised world. Certain manufactured goods require sophisticated marketing and distribution networks in the country of sale. Experience goods – those whose performance adequacy cannot be determined visually prior to purchase – require an after-sales service system, possibly involving a credible warranty and/or a network of repair outlets. The creation of such a network constitutes a formidable barrier to exports of such goods for firms with their roots in developing nations. Marketing and distribution activities are the most closely related to the culture of the country of final use, and a developing country would be at its most serious disadvantage in such activities in an affluent nation. By combining the production process with the marketing and distribution activity under a single *aegis,* MNCs can achieve economies of vertical integration (so-called internalisation efficiencies) in production *and* in combining production abroad with an established marketing and distribution network in the importing country. The effect of such combinations would be to enhance considerably the range of products which southern economies might expect to export to industrialised nations in the absence of barriers to imports. The more willing Third World nations are to attract direct foreign investment (and the creation of export zones and the offer of investment inducements for investment in backward regions both suggest that Third World nations perceive foreign direct investment in a favourable light), the greater is the potential range and volume of imports into the industrialised countries under the auspices of MNCs. The demand profile will be raised.

The weight of the evidence suggests that the institution of free trade would present serious problems of adjustment for the industrialised world because the surge in the capacity of exports of sophisticated manufactured goods will have the net effect of displacing low-skilled workers (Aho and Orr, 1981). Given the constraints which apply to the supply profiles in industrialised nations in all time frames, there is a strong likelihood that the adjustment costs of a free-trade policy would prove to be chronic. Many industrialised nations, particularly those with large numbers of disadvantaged ethnic minorities, are likely already to have more workers constrained in the category of low-skilled than can be employed or upgraded in the medium run (Johnson, 1978). The possibility that a nation will face serious, chronic adjustment costs with free trade merits serious attention.

It is possible, in abstract theory at least, to solve the problems of the unemployed with generous unemployment transfer payments. Hindley and Nicolaides (1983, p. 51) seem to suggest such a policy. Curzon Price (1981) is explicit that displacement should be generously financed, although she does not conceive of the problem in terms of chronic adjustment. On the other hand, the report on conditions in the Netherlands (Nordheimer, 1983) suggests that 'relatively generous' social welfare payments do not eliminate discontent on the part of the unemployed. The usual outlet for low-skilled workers, in the eyes of adjustment optimists and free-trade advocates, is the service sector, which by its nature tends to be protected against international competition. This easy and comfortable solution is deprived of its strength by the wave of labour-saving technology that parallels the surge of southern export capacity.

Hager (1982) puts the problem into a much broader context. Concerned primarily with the potential impact of North–South trade, Hager views the question on the basis of the inequality of income-distribution in terms of what he calls a 'security bargain', and what will be referred to more generally here as 'the social contract'. Hager's argument is that, prior to the ability of southern nations to invade northern markets with sophisticated manufactured goods,

Western Europe found answers to problems which had occupied domestic and international politics for a century: the class war seemed settled once and for all by redistributions of income and the introduction of contractual elements in the labour 'market', which narrowed the gap between wage earners and the middle classes.

This state of affairs, according to Hager, created a calm (political) pole in a world of conflict.

Concentrating more on the introduction of the new labour-saving technologies (Chips and Robots), Leontief addresses the possibility of severe surpluses of labour and pays little attention to the level of skills of the unemployed, although tacitly these do seem to be concentrated in the lower levels of skills in conformity with Canterbery's model. Leontief (1982) suggests that the increase in real income that derives from the introduction of new technologies be mandatorily taken out in shortened working weeks. He is proposing job–sharing as a solution to an otherwise insoluble problem.

For many nations the restructuring of the social contract will be traumatic. Old, devoutly-held values and traditions will have to go by the board. The so-called Puritan 'work ethic' will have to be renounced not only by the permanently unemployed, but also by those high-caste people who remain employed (cf. Leontief, 1982, p. 194). Claims on old-age support will have to be redrafted to allow for the problem of the permanently unemployed, or more correctly, those who are permanently underemployed by traditional standards. The social contract will have to be established anew in order that it may conform to the new reality. None of this is likely to be achieved quickly or easily when people who have made their way under the old conditions resist political innovations which recognise the new reality. It will be a time for political leadership, and it must be hoped that a politician of sufficient calibre will arrive without the need for plunging western economies into disarray. Too often leadership of the quality required emerges only from the ashes of economic despair.

III   INEQUALITIES IN SUBSISTENCE INCOME

The possibility of accelerated adjustment costs being incurred by the North (Chapter 4) derives from the rate of growth of export capacity of sophisticated manufactured goods from southern nations. The possibility of chronic adjustment costs follows from the integration of global labour markets so that the marginal worker in the industrialised bloc is unable to find employment at subsistence income. The larger the volume of imports into the North of low-skilled labour-intensive manufactures, the greater the likelihood that chronic adjustment costs will be incurred. If the cost of low-skilled labour is less in southern economies than in the North then a greater volume of trade will be seen than would be compatible with equal money wages for unskilled labour in the two blocs. This section suggests that there are several reasons for expecting that the money costs of unskilled labour (subsistence income) will be lower in the South than in the North under conditions of free trade. The likelihood of chronic adjustment costs is greater than a simple analysis in terms of the factor-price equalisation model would imply.

The motive power of international trade is differences in costs of production (in the absence of trade or in the presence of impediments to trade). Costs must be measured in some international numeraire and are translated from the domestic currencies at the going rates of exchange. The effect of different costs of low-skilled (marginal) labour on the pattern of trade can be seen in a more familiar context by assuming that one nation subsidises its exports. The volume of exports increases, more foreign exchange is earned and more imports are financed. The exports will reflect the factor composition that underlies comparative advantage so that if the South subsidises exports in the absence of man-made impediments to trade, the North will import more goods which utilise low-skilled labour intensively.

The factors which will contribute to the lower money wage in southern economies can be analysed under three headings: (1) price differences in non-tradables; (2) different histories of and concern with worker safety; and (3) different social concepts of subsistence. All of these will be mutually–reinforcing suggesting that the money wage of the marginal worker will be lower in the South in full equilibrium.

1. Real income depends upon money income and on the price of goods bought with that income. If international trade is not impeded except through inescapable costs of transportation, the prices of internationally traded goods (direct taxes aside) can be considered to be almost equal in the two countries or blocs so that differences in money incomes will closely reflect differences in real incomes if all incomes are spent on tradable goods. However, domestic goods constitute a large proportion of consumption in practice, and the ratio of domestic to imported goods in the consumption package will probably be closely and negatively related to income. The purchasing power of money wage rates in different countries will tend therefore to vary most importantly for

lower-skilled workers.

Domestic goods will tend to be priced lower in southern economies than in northern economies because of what may be termed the laggard working of the market. Labour markets are not perfect, and clearly there is the possibility of market segmentation, in terms of workers employed in tradable-goods industries which experience the pressure of wages directly (either through the competition of imports or the demand for exports) and those employed in what Hager (1982) calls 'the sheltered sector'. To be sure, Hager is thinking of northern economies when he derives his expression but 'sheltered' is an appropriate |term. The domestic-goods industries are sheltered from the effects of international trade by means of transportation costs. In rich economies, this sheltering can generate strong market imperfections – particular professional requirements and craft unions which are able to exploit their control over labour supply to those areas. The cost of domestic goods will be likely to be substantially higher in rich economies than in southern economies. Workers in the sheltered sector in northern economies will be able to resist market pressures and enjoy quasi-rents.[7] In southern economies, workers in the domestic-goods sector will find themselves still supporting the burden of excess population and unable to enjoy the pull-effects of increased demand in the tradable-goods sectors. The full force of the market mechanism can only be achieved if full employment of labour (and other factors) prevails in the economies concerned, but even that force can be blunted by the strength of unions in northern economies. The authoritative empirical work on this subject has been conducted by Usher (1963a and 1963b) on real wages in Thailand in contrast with real wages in Britain. The comparison based on the value of money wages measured in terms of an international numeraire and computed without reference to expenditure patterns and the role of domestic goods far exceeded the differential when domestic goods and expenditure patterns were taken into account.

In terms of Figure 5.1, the effect of domestic goods is to reduce the subsistence money wage below (flatter than) WW so that I_L will lie closer to R_L in a southern economy than in a northern one. The larger volume of international trade that is induced by the disparity in the cost of domestic goods changes the composite good in both countries and shifts the isoquant, the two ridge lines and the isocline to the left in a northern economy. This effect increases the likelihood of chronic adjustment costs.

    Tradition cannot be neglected. If northern economies have come to accept a working week which is significantly shorter than that which is traditional in the southern bloc, then the disparity in real wage *rates* is enhanced. Once again, market pressures may be expected to result in a shortening of the working week in the southern economy, and a comparable lengthening in northern economies, but this adjustment will be effected only slowly.

2. Just as tradition in terms of the accepted length of the working week will accentuate diffferences in wage-*rates* (but not necessarily in wages), so too can the accepted social norm about working conditions affect labour productivity. In northern economies where workers were once scarce and where affluence enabled legislatures to lay down high standards of worker safety, productivity per person-hour will be less than that of a comparably skilled and supported worker in a foreign country in which safety regulations are much more lax. The disparity in efficiency wages (labour cost per unit of output) will be further enhanced. Workers in southern economies will have higher productivity and lower nominal wage rates than their counterparts in the North.

3. Despite Meade's concept of welfare-subsistence, the notion of subsistence income is not a precise one. It may be possible to determine for an individual some level of physiological subsistence implying the maintenance of the body. However, given the wide variation in physical attributes, even such a limited concept of subsistence could not be determined for a working population. In addition there exist the questions of familial structure and the number of dependents who also have to be maintained at 'subsistence level' by the wage of a single worker.

    Tradition will play a powerful role in the determination of the meaning of subsistence. In countries used to the existence of surplus labour, the meaning of subsistence will be likely to imply a much lower level of existence than will be true for countries which have at one time been short of labour, and have had the opportunity to introduce humanitarian considerations into the narrow scope of formal economic policy.

    All the factors considered here will tend to increase the probability that northern economies would be likely to have to submit to chronic adjustment costs if free trade were to become dominant. The main source of such a severe dislocation lies in North–South trade. It is possible that with the advent of labour-saving technology with the capacity to create chronic adjustment costs, trade within the northern bloc might also lead to chronic adjustment burdens for some nations (see Chapter 8).

IV SUMMARY

The rapid and startling increase in the capacity of the newly–industrialising countries and their successor nations (Lorenz, 1983) to supply both standardised and sophisticated differentiated manufactures to the industrialised world has exposed that bloc to the possibility of permanent structural unemployment (chronic adjustment costs). By virtue of bumping and the direct impact on the derived demand for skills of the new pattern of international trade flows, any surplus of workers in the industrialised countries will be concentrated in the low-skilled categories. These workers are likely to correspond quite closely to the disadvantaged members of the societies in, at least, the short and medium runs. In the very long run, when the genetic constraint is the crucial limiting factor, the composition of surplus workers by social group cannot be foretold. The ability of the industrialised countries to respond to this threat will depend upon the magnitude of the problem and upon the ability of these countries to develop effective skill-acquisition programmes. However, even if limits to skill acquisitions are not the operative constraint, the problem is likely to exist as long as workers in Third World countries can produce goods more cheaply that the industrial nations, and as long as some form of Say's Law does not provide adequate demand for labour in the high-cost industrial nations. No one can tell to what degree increased income in low-income countries will be returned to the industrial nations in the form of demand for their exports, but there can be no assurance that this happy state of affairs can be relied upon to develop quickly, and nor will such a state of affairs eliminate the labour cost advantage of low-income countries where the history of past poverty will exert a lingering impact on both the work standards employed in those countries and on the local price of domestic (non-tradable) goods.

The possibility of chronic adjustment costs as a result of new patterns of international trade will be reinforced by the new wave of labour-saving technologies which are sweeping the world. It may well turn out that the new technologies may prove to be the more serious cause of permanent structural unemployment. In any event, the two phenomena will reinforce each other.

Some optimists see no difficulty in having the industrial world respond to the increased capacity to export of countries with large populations and high rates of population growth. Krueger (1980) suggests that:

> economic growth of the OECD countries has been accompanied by (as well as caused by, at least in a simplistic sense) a drastic shift in the educational and occupational composition of the labour force: unskilled, illiterate workers are really a thing of the past. As the labour force's training and skills become more productive, the real wage increases, since men are becoming scarcer relative to machines and other resources.

Contrast this with the comment reported in Terkel (1979) by a factory manager in Lancashire, England:

> What industry would you suggest these people are retrained to go into? Mention half a dozen expanding industries to me in this country at the moment. What are we supposed to do – all become astronauts? All become scientists? There are people in this factory who are very happy with the work they're doing, working in an environment that suits them. They are not cut out to be academics, they're not cut out to be astronauts, they are not cut out to be technologists.

The problem is made potentially more serious by the ability of MNCs to transfer the technology from the developed to the Third World nations. The effect of the pattern of trade is to integrate labour markets with (erstwhile) surplus labour with nations with (erstwhile) labour shortages. The effect of the new technologies will be to reduce the amount of labour demanded per unit of output (and particularly low-skilled labour) in both blocs. Optimum population (and this concept is a particularly tricky one) will inevitably be substantially reduced in both blocs. If the authorities have no direct, and possibly negligible indirect control over net reproduction rates, then the stage is set for either a period of massive political and economic restructuring or for catastrophe.

The two major sources of chronic adjustment costs are likely to prove to be mutually reinforcing. New trade patterns are more likely to create a mismatch of the skill-mix in the northern economies and the new labour-saving technologies may well begin by reinforcing the effects of the new trade patterns, but may finish by creating excess labour without regard to the level of skills available. What of protection against imports under such circumstances? Protection will be able to reduce the speed of, and perhaps prevent, the effect of enhanced export capacity by southern nations causing chronic adjustment costs as a result of the mismatch in skills demanded and supplied. Protection may, then, provide the authorities in the industrialised world with badly needed time for adjustment. Given the potentially devastating restructuring of society's concepts of normalcy which could be required, time, if efficiently used, could prove very valuable.[8] However, protection will only play a major identifiable role if new trade patterns are the dominant cause of potential chronic unemployment. If technology is the more important force, as well it may be, then protection will provide only a short breathing space in which to cope better with the socio-economic upheaval.

The problem addressed in this chapter is likely to prove the dominant challenge facing western democracies in the rest of this century. Its impact will require the destruction of many time-honoured and cherished ideals and received wisdom on which the material well-being of the industrialised nations has been built.

6 Impasse in North–South Policy Formulation

The preceding three chapters have shown that the analytic base underlying the free-trade argument is not appropriate to situations in which the underlying conditions change at a rate which exceeds the capability of nations to adjust benignly. A free-trade or passive posture may not be the best policy for industrialised countries in turbulent periods. Moreover the process of change could be sufficiently severe that it invokes episodes of anarchy (as in British coalmines and the French steel industry in March and early April 1984). The process of adjustment and adaptation cannot be considered independently of the political process.

The root of the problem is the changed character of North–South trade from one of complementary trade in which each bloc exports what the other bloc cannot produce or cannot produce in quantities necessary for self-sufficiency. This is trade in non-competitive imports. The surge of capacity in the Third World to supply manufactures of some sophistication to northern countries has transformed the pattern of trade into substitute trade whereby exports from the South compete with and displace production in the North (Lorenz, 1982). Yet the North has a very real interest in the continued prosperity and development of the South in addition to any moral concern with the diminution of poverty in those countries. North–South trade is still complementary to an important degree, and the South constitutes a very large market for very high-technology manufactured goods. The North also relies on the South for the supply of many of its basic commodities. The solution to the Third World debt crisis requires that debtor nations have the opportunity to earn convertible currencies so that indebtedness may be reduced or debt-bearing capacity may be increased. Northern prosperity will also release the severity of austerity imposed upon debtor nations as an ingredient in balance-of-payments adjustment policies. Finally, and perhaps the most important aspect of all, world peace will probably have a better chance for survival in a well-functioning, prosperous world.

The observed success of export-led growth may be the result of the exploitation of a window of opportunity during which the developed nations were able to undergo adjustment without serious cost. Provided that latent capacity to adjust existed, the benefits to northern nations clearly outweighed the cost. This is the essence of the traditional theory. But if the adjustment process was benign in its early stages, social costs grew as the latent capacity for adjustment was exhausted. Political pressures for protection grew. If industrialised countries cannot continue to accept increases in manufactured imports from the South, the export-led growth may prove to be an abortive strategy and Prebisch's concept of import substitution may come once again into favour. Section I develops a simple theory of adjustment and adjustment policy and integrates that theory with the underlying relationships which impede adjustment, and which, in turn, develop political pressures.

Section II presents the argument that one of the impediments to intelligent policy formulation in this area of North–South trade relations is the failure of politicians and economists in both the North and South, explicitly to confront the reality of an actual or potential clash of interests.

Section III considers the problem of the division of adjustment strains within the North. It confronts the question of the desirability of intra-bloc cooperation as a means of improving the capacity of the northern bloc to accept ever-increasing amounts of imports. Finally, Section IV examines some other policy options which might usefully be considered as a means of continuing the viability of export-led growth.[1]

I THE EVOLUTION OF SOCIAL COSTS AND POLITICAL PRESSURES

The crucial weakness of the free-trade model in any analysis of adjustment is that it neglects the possibility that political pressures against the continued growth of imports will evolve automatically and grow over time to the point that free trade is no longer feasible. This process has been evident in the 1970s and early 1980s. Hager (1982) has suggested that the more severe the costs and the more widespread their effects, the more likely is political opposition to imports (and to the attendant job losses) to develop and to lead to *ad hoc* protectionism. Such a scenario will be likely to constitute the worst of all possible worlds as 'panic protectionism' becomes the result of a failure to confront the clash of interests.

Countries facing the need for adjustment have four categories of policies at their disposal: adjustment-suppressing policies which eliminate the need for adjustment by refusing to accept any social costs in the interests of a well-functioning global economy; adjustment-retarding policies which slow down the rate of change imposed on their economies by reducing the magnitude of the disturbance; adjustment-facilitating policies which are designed to improve the capacity of the home economy to accept the new underlying conditions; and adjustment-effecting policies which involve intervention to eliminate a structural feature in the home economy which is blocking the process of adjustment. Straightforward commercial policy would constitute suppressive policies; phase-out protection would be a retarding policy; improvements in information flows and increased availability of retraining facilities would be adjustment-facilitating policies; and wage freezes in an industry with a wage premium would be an adjustment-effecting measure. Adjustment-facilitating policies are likely to be long-term measures since they involve some structural change in the economy, and because in many instances the efficacy of such measures has not been great. So-called 'positive adjustment policies' (Michalski, 1983) would comprise adjustment-facilitating and adjustment-effecting policies. Conditional protection involving phase-out protection with an adjustment-effecting measure would also constitute a positive policy.

Combining these concepts of different kinds of policies with the mismatches of the supply and demand profiles of the national labour force is instructive because it shows how the success of export-led growth could become a transitory phenomenon. The essence of the problem is that export-led growth imposes push-adjustment on the North and this type of adjustment encounters both recessionary tendencies and the need for upgrading of the skill level of the labour force. In the terminology developed in Chapter 5, export-led growth will generate a demand profile higher than the supply profile.

Figure 6.1 shows how social costs of adjustment vary with the rate of increase of the ratio of imports to gross national product. Curve 1 shows the relationship which may have existed in the North in 1968.

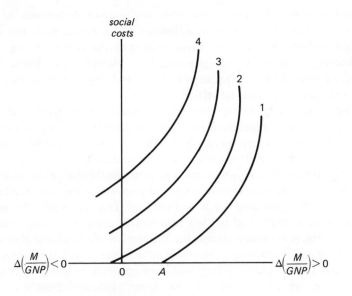

FIGURE 6.1 *The determination of social costs of adjustment*

Benign adjustment was possible for an increase in the import ratio of less than O*A*. The curve has positive first and second derivatives because of the increasing difficulty of upgrading workers in the short period, and it becomes vertical when chronic adjustment costs are incurred. As the latent capacity to adjust becomes used up (in response to the original surge in imports), the curve shifts upwards and to the left (curve 2). Ultimately a constant rate of increase of imports (to GNP) will induce accelerated costs of adjustment if there are no automatic improvements in the supply profile (caused, for example, by improved training availability). The passage of time will continue to shift the curves upwards (to curves 3 and 4) indicating that accelerated costs of adjustment can be inflicted by a constant ratio of imports to GNP. Ultimately, as the labour force approaches its maximum-attainable supply profile, the curves become vertical to the left of the vertical axis (with a diminishing but positive ratio of imports to GNP). Adjustment-suppressive policies prevent the ratio from increasing and may even decrease it. Adjustment-retarding measures also push the economy to the left relative to where it would otherwise have been. The magnitude of a disturbance is measured by the consequent rightward movement and the severity of the disturbance by the size of the first and second derivatives of the individual curves. *Per contra,* adjustment-facilitating measures or a period without pressures to adjust will shift the curves to the right indicating a capacity for adjustment at lower cost. (Note that a reinforcing domestic shock will reduce the capacity to adjust and will shift the curves to the left.)

There are likely to be two main sources of political pressure: workers whose displacement involves a reduction in their incomes in such new jobs as are available to them; and the social costs of adjustment measured in terms of the amount and duration of unemployment. Workers who must downgrade themselves to find new employment will exert as much political pressure as they can muster in the hope off avoiding such a pay cut. This is much the· same mechanism as leads laid off workers to find temporary employment (and bumping someone else in the process) while retaining the hope that they will ultimately be reabsorbed back into their original industry. In that industry they will have enjoyed a wage premium or will have earned a return on some industry-specific skills. Unemployment will also give rise to political pressure from workers who see little hope of alternative employment and seek merely to regain a reliable future income stream. This kind of political pressure will require some minimum critical mass before it becomes effective, and may become effective only with a pronounced lag: then, when protectionist forces gain the upper hand, their impact is the more devastating. Adjustment-suppressing and adjustment-retarding measures will become commonplace and will be likely to be more restrictive than 'best' policy would countenance. It is to be hoped that, under such circumstances, legislatures will recognise the problems for what they are, will countenance (and enact) adjustment as well as adjustment-effecting measures, and will avoid permanent (or *sine die*) adjustment suppression.

Natural (exogenous) supply-side effects cannot be disregarded. If the existence of chronic adjustment costs generates some upgrading of school children in terms of their educational achievements, or if local governments increase the efficiency of the school systems, the capacity to adjust will be enhanced. If poor people, with only crowded and inferior school facilities available to them, reproduce more quickly then the problem is aggravated. Like adjustment-facilitating measures, these natural phenomena are likely to become effective only after a long period of time.

The danger of indiscriminate or *ad hoc* protectionism is that adjustment-suppressing measures will be imposed without reference to the process of adjustment over time and in response only to the ability of those damaged by imports to generate political action. The long-run prospects of the protected industry and the adaptation of the economy will be ignored. The net result of this will be an economy which loses its capability to adapt to internal as well as external change, and which will lose the growth impetus that comes from the emergence of new industries (cf. Walter, 1981–2). In Michalski's terms (1983), the economy will lose the 'virtuous circle of micro-economic flexibility and macro-economic stability' and will become increasingly prone to inflation and/or unemployment as resources become locked into low-growth sectors.

II NEGLECTING TO CONFRONT THE CLASH OF INTERESTS

Despite the seeming inevitability of politically-induced protection in response to adjustment costs, spokespeople for the South seem to continue to assume that free trade, or at least preferential trade, is a right. In the North, politicians and bureaucrats (as well as economists) countenance the desirability of absolutely free trade in their rhetoric at the same time as their pragmatic instincts lead them to develop a myriad of ingenious arrangements which interfere with the free flow of goods and services without irremediably impairing the purity of their intellectual position. In April 1984 the Reagan Administration in the US, whose rhetoric in favour of absolute freedom to trade and to invest has been unconstrained, announced measures on 27 March 1984 to exclude from the duty-free preference list (under the Generalised System of Preferences or GSP) imports that in 1983 were valued at $11.9 billion (*New York Times,* 28 March 1984). In addition to the elimination of preferential treatment accorded to goods under the GSP, such measures as 'orderly marketing arrangements' and 'voluntary export restraints' serve as simple euphemisms for straightforward quotas. It is the argument of this section that the failure to recognise (and confront) the existence of either accelerated or chronic adjustment costs results in representatives of both blocs avoiding the central issue which precludes the solution claimed by the South and proclaimed by the North.

The willingness of informed people in the North to neglect the clash of interests can be illustrated by reference to the 'McFadzean Report'

(1981), as well as to the Multi-Fibre Arrangement (MFA).[2] The willingness of the South to ignore the costs to the North of free trade and free technology transfer to the South can be deduced from Roffe (1977).

The McFadzean Report serves to redress what the authors of the document see as an excessively interventionist, aid-oriented prescription by the Brandt Commission on the issues of the international aspects of economic development.[3] Perhaps the only area of agreement of the two sets of prescriptions is that free and open access to northern markets is fundamental to the development process. The McFadzean Report presents the argument for allowing private enterprise a major role in the process of economic development, and in the process endorses the export-oriented, outward-looking development strategies which were espoused with considerable success by Brazil and Mexico and, in particular, by the 'Four Little Dragons' (Hong Kong, Korea, Singapore and Taiwan). The report also emphasises the role of MNCs which 'have enabled the developing countries to market manufactured goods abroad by producing goods up to international quality standards and in adequate supply, also in providing distribution outlets in foreign markets' (McFadzean, 1981, p. 25).

An unfortunate and inevitable consequence of an adversary approach to the formulation of economic policy is that it prevents protagonists from raising points which weaken their arguments. Any growth of manufactured exports by the bloc of developing nations will, growth effects aside, require adjustment in the developed countries which constitute the markets of final use. The McFadzean Report's major weakness is the lack of analysis of the implications of such adjustment. The outward-looking development strategy relies on passive openness on the part of the bloc of developed nations. The political difficulties which may follow from a surge of imports are acknowledged, but are dissolved in an aura of Panglossian optimism (pp. 79–81):

> There is no denying the political problems in such a course for the governments of developed countries. But electorates need to be properly informed of the costs and benefits of different courses of action. This is a matter for leadership and of fulfilling the information function of government.

The same failure to confront the clash of interests is evident in a report on the problem of discriminatory protection of textiles and apparel (or clothing)[4] encompassed under the MFA written by six distinguished international economists (Curzon *et al.*, 1981). The report, 'MFA Forever?' focuses on the protectionism in textiles and apparel as a vehicle for launching the broader argument for a complete dismantling of complex schemes of protection used by developed nations against imports from the South. The choice of the MFA as a vehicle for analysis of discrimination is natural since the MFA is the most tortuous of all the formalised schemes of discriminations.[5] It was due for renewal at the end of 1981, and the inherent bilateral agreements between importers and suppliers were due for renewal in 1982. One of the possible features of the renewal was that there would be a restriction of import growth to the rate experienced by the market for textiles and/or clothing in the developed market. This would freeze market shares for the life of the agreement, and would represent a very important precedent effectively precluding the reallocation of resources out of the textile and clothing industries in developed countries and of the production of these labour-intensive goods to developing countries (Curzon *et al.*, 1981, pp. 6–7).[6] The proposed process is uncomfortably close to the hodge-podge of protective devices devised by the European and US Steel industries in which only the interests of the endangered industry are considered. This practice has been identified by Walter (1979) as 'sectoral protection'. The thrust of 'MFA Forever?' is contained in Hugh Corbet's preface (p. viii):

> If the liberal principles of the international trading system, as expressed in the General Agreement on Tariffs and Trade (GATT) are to be preserved for the benefit of all, merely verbal assertions by the governments of developed countries of their commitment to these principles are not enough. Governments have to demonstrate that they mean what they say. They have to repudiate the precedents for departures from those principles. They have to convey a signal to the unprotected industries. In short, they have to start dismantling restrictive trade measures such as the Multi-Fibre Arrangement, 'voluntary' export restraint agreements, sectoral pacts of a cartel character and non-tariff devices which destroy trade.

The report addresses the possibility of continued renewals of the arrangement and argues the case against a renewal that does not contain the seeds of its own destruction (pp. 37–9):

If there is to be escape [from the MFA], then there has to be a plan for it. A commitment should be made to liberalisation in accordance with a timetable, just as there was during the formation of the European Community, or during major rounds of international trade liberalisation. This timetable should be long enough for the producers to plan orderly 'exit', where necessary, while enjoying the benefits of protection in the short run. It is particularly important that the timetable be seen as inviolate ... In practice ... unilateral liberalisation is almost inconceivable. It is only within the framework of an international agreement to liberalise that there is any hope of the desired changes (being instituted).... [T]he method ... might be to agree on the renewal of the MFA for a longer period than four years, but [to] establish certain clear guidelines on future bilateral restrictions. In particular, the growth rates (of imports) permitted for the first five years or so might be negligible, but thereafter any bilateral agreement would have to embody steadily accelerating growth rates year by year until all quantitative limits were abolished, perhaps ten years from now. From then on, problems in textiles and clothing would be dealt with in accordance with the general rules on safeguard protection on a non-discriminatory basis, and if possible, by the use of tariffs rather than quotas.

'MFA Forever?' gives explicit recognition to the existence of adjustment costs by building into its recommended policy a phase-out period of protection (senile industry protection). In this aspect, it is far more realistic than most of the arguments made for freer, non-discriminatory trade. But the report locks itself into the impasse by failing to confront the need for positive adjustment policies to assist in maintaining the burden of adjustment costs at some socially tolerable level. In the absence of such measures, it is very unlikely that the promised accelerated rates of growth of imports would be permitted to take place. In essence, the report assumes that a decentralised set of factor markets will, if aided by phase-out protection, successfully resolve the reallocation problem. This assumption leads to exaggerated statements such as (Curzon *et al.*, 1981, p. 19):

> Since the private losses are transient, while the social costs for the misallocation of resources are permanent, it makes no sense to renew and extend the restrictive arrangements governing trade in textiles and clothing indefinitely. *It is safe to say that if restrictions*

*had not been introduced, virtually all workers and capitalists now
engaged would be enjoying as high (if not higher) incomes in other
activities as they do in textiles and clothing today.*
   [Italics added]

The assumption that a system of decentralised markets will, given time
effect the needed adjustments, and find better paying occupations for
the workers displaced, is heroic. Certainly the assertion assumes the
absence of serious recession and sits uneasily with conditions
prevailing in 1983. It is symptomatic of blind faith in the workings of
decentralised markets: it makes no reference to the limitations of the
work force to absorb capital or to the possibility that reinforcing
disturbances will aggravate the task at hand.

   When the argument for non-discrimination is couched in terms of
the MFA, there is a basic point which must be made clear. The two
product groups (textiles and clothing) included in the MFA have
traditionally been yoked together under the same protective
legislation, but the two industries are widely different in their need for
protection. Textiles is a capital– and technologically-intensive
industry, while clothing relies predominantly on low-skilled labour.
This distinction runs through the report like a leitmotiv, particularly
when data on market shares and trade volumes are cited. But the
report fails clearly to distinguish between the two industries when
making its policy recommendations.

   The report cites (and rejects with varying degrees of intensity) nine
arguments for the continuation of protection under the MFA (Curzon
et al., 1981, pp. 8–9):

(a) that the 'low-cost' exporters threaten the extinction of a major
industry.
(b) that there is no alternative employment for a large section of the
labour force employed in these industries in industrialised
countries, especially because the industry is concentrated in
declining regions and employs disadvantaged segments of the
population.
(c) that defence of the textile and clothing industries is necessary for
industrial survival.
(d) that 'real developing countries' do not benefit – only the four
Asian newly-industrialising countries. (NICs).
(e) that the people of the exporting countries do not benefit – only
capitalists.

(f) that the success of developing countries is caused by subsidies and exploitation of labour.

(g) that the developing countries protect their own markets and do not deserve open markets.

(h) that the 'burden' of cheap imports is unfairly distributed among the industrialised countries.

(i) that the clothing industry warrants national defence protection.

This book is concerned with the validity of argument (b) that accelerated (or chronic) costs of adjustment can impose long-term unemployment on displaced workers in social settings which do not countenance the underlying causes of the unemployment. Because the emphasis of the book is on *rates* of adjustment, argument (h) is also germane. If one nation in the northern bloc is able to restrict imports, it sloughs the burdens of adjustment off on to other members of the bloc. This problem involves both equity considerations and raises doubts about the ability of international cooperation to survive. Further if costs of adjustment are an increasing function of the speed of adjustment, total costs of adjustment within the bloc will be minimised when the rate of adjustment is equal in all countries, and a sloughing-off process will increase the total costs.[7]

The report's main weakness is its neglect of the costs of adjustment for the clothing industry with its intensive reliance upon workers with low general skills which can be utilised in other industries. (It is possible for workers to become quite highly skilled in certain industry-specific activities, which can be mastered mainly through experience, and still have very low skill levels when the question is one of transference to another industry.) By implying that no positive adjustment policies are necessary for the clothing industry, the report, despite its recognition of the positive aspects of phase-out protection, reinforces the impasse in world policy formulation.

There exists one important facet of the displacement of low-skilled workers which merits attention. This is the hypothesis that displacement of workers in low-skilled labour-intensive industries comes about inevitably: if international trade flows do not eliminate the jobs for low-skilled workers, machines will do so. This proposition antedates the advent of Chips and Robots, and is based essentially on the fact that low-skilled labour is, in industrialised nations, an extremely costly input. This may be due to the cost of non-tradable goods and the protection of the agricultural sectors in many industrialised countries. Certainly, machines have replaced low-skilled workers in clothing (and in similar industries such as shoe manufacture) and the number of displacements (or non-replacements) attributable to new machines seems to surpass those attributable to imports of clothing from the developing world. One of the better known studies testing this hypothesis is that of Krueger (1980). Krueger concludes that 'the dislocations generated by imports into the US do not appear to have been an identifiably major source of structural change' (1980, p. 240), but she recognises that it may not be legitimate to extrapolate these results into the future. Krueger's sample covers the years 1970 to 1976 (the year when the US finally introduced its own version of the Generalised System of Preferences) and her major tests are based on two-digit data, although she runs some tests on four-digit data, and these results do not contradict the results with two-digit data. The major surge in US imports of manufactures from the South took place after 1976 (see Table 6.1 below). Krueger's analysis does not countenance the heterogeneity of labour and pressupposes (probably correctly at that time) that the economy was capable of absorbing relatively small numbers of displaced workers without undue difficulty. It is possible that Krueger underestimates the effect of imports on employment by assuming that the shift to more capital–intensive methods of production was spontaneous and unrelated to import pressures. When the cost of capital falls relative to the cost of low-skilled labour, input substitution is a natural result compatible with the cost–minimisation criterion for survival in competitive industries. If low-skilled labour is also the factor of production in which the US has the biggest comparative disadvantage, goods which use low-skilled labour intensively will be those goods in which the nation has the greatest comparative disadvantage (Gray, 1979, Appendix to Chapter 5). Import pressures may have been the motivating force for adopting greater capital intensity as firms searched for survival in the face of pressure from imports. Under these circumstances, concerns with the welfare of displaced workers by erstwhile employers become minimal. In the longer run, these forces are probably inevitable in the absence of government intervention. But, as Curzon *et al.* (1981, p. 17) correctly point out, governments should not protect industries with the expectation that these industries can become competitive with imports, and particularly should not bring about protection by subsidising the cost of capital to such industries. Such a strategy will allow the industry to survive with more capital and less labour and to make only a token contribution, if any, to the problem of adjustment in the labour markets. The essence of the problem is the lesser mobility of labour than of capital (and in terms of chronic costs, the zero mobility of labour) and the intent of intervention is to minimise the social costs of adjustment. Perpetuating the existence of an internationally–inefficient industry can be warranted only on the grounds of *force majeure*. It is not permissible to forget the purpose of protection and to consider the protection of an industry for its own sake as adequate. The purpose of protection lies in the factor and not in the product markets.

III THE DIVISION OF ADJUSTMENT STRAINS

As indicated in the preceding section and confirmed by Figure 6.2, there is an argument in favour of equalising the strains of adjustment imposed on each of the northern industrialised countries. Clearly this argument lacks the strength to make it an absolute criterion because of the different (latent) capacities for adjustment within nations at any one time and because of the differences in spontaneous domestic shocks which nations are experiencing. But the argument is strong enough to suggest that any serious inequalities in the rate of growth of imports to GNP among industrialised nations should raise the question of one nation or more not bearing the social optimal burden (that is, their 'fair share' of the North's total burden). Figure 6.2 shows the social cost/change in the import ratio relationship for a representative northern country. If all northern countries had the same relationship as indicated by the curve, then there would be a strong argument for equalising the absolute increase in the ratio of imports of manufactures to GNP as a means of minimising total (northern) social costs of adjustment. Consider two countries with ratios of imports to GNP of b and c respectively. The social costs imposed are Ob' and Oc'. If the two countries were of equal size, by having the country with the import ratio of Ob increase its import ratio to Oa and by having the second country reduce its ratio to Oa as well, total social costs of adjustment would be reduced from $(Ob' + Oc')$ to $2(Oa')$. This argument derives from the shape of the cost/import ratio curve which reflects the propositions which underlie Figure 6.1. Costs of adjustment increase with the ratio of imports to GNP (the size of the shock) at an increasing rate. The policy statement that all nations should be subjected to equal adjustment strains is weakened by two considerations: the measure of strain is imperfect (as

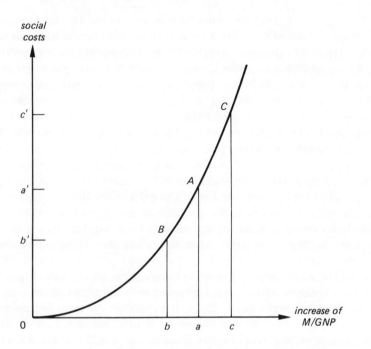

FIGURE 6.2   *The distribution of and total costs of adjustment*

is considered below); and while the shape of the curve may be common to all nations, the position and the slope are not. Countries differ in their abilities to adapt and, in all likelihood, the impact of a particular increase in export capacity by Third World nations may have quite different effects on different countries.

The second important aspect of the effect of export-led growth (and the concomitant high rates of increase in the capacity of the South to export manufactures) is the interdependence of the magnitude of the effects on individual northern countries. Consider the possibility that one country manages by dint of non-transparent commercial policies to reduce the pressure of imports on its domestic industries. The exporters, seeking markets where they can find them, will increase the concentration of their sales efforts in the other members of the North – in those markets which have not been impeded by government actions. In terms of Figure 6.2, efforts by one country to reduce its ratio from Oa to Ob may result in greater efforts being made in other markets with the result that ratios in those countries increase (if the first country were as large as the sum of other members of the bloc, the ratio of other members would increase to O*c*). This is a somewhat different concept of trade diversion than that used in an analysis of the effects of economic integration but the mechanics are the same. The possibility of export diversion becomes even more important when experience goods are being exported. Experience goods require that the exporter establish a marketing and distribution organisation in the country of final sale. These organisations are costly to establish and involve large amounts of fixed costs. A firm will be more likely to invest the money and the effort in a country in which impediments to imports do not exist and in which such impediments are unlikely to be imposed arbitrarily or capriciously in the future. Thus a nation with a structured and formal system of appeal against import competition marked by the ability of the exporter to make counter-arguments, is likely to prove a more attractive long–term market than a country which may use bureaucratic obstacles in a seemingly capricious way to curb imports.[8]

All these arguments, if they are to be used at all as guides for policy, need a measure of the strain imposed on the industrialised country. The measure chosen is the absolute increase in the ratio of imports of manufactures to GNP and has been used in Figures 6.1 and 6.2. The advantage of the ratio is that it makes an automatic allowance for inflation, economic growth and recession. The ratio does not measure the actual strain imposed – that depends upon the severity of the shock and the capacity to adjust in the individual nation and is subsumed in the shape and position of the curve in Figure 6.2 – but it does provide a good indication of the potential strain. The ratio covers manufactured goods (SITC categories 5–8, excepting 67 and 68).

Tables 6.1 and 6.2 show the ratios for six industrialised nations for the years 1968–80. Table 6.2 excludes SITC 8 which encompasses both apparel (clothing) and footwear along with miscellaneous manufactures ranging from furniture and household appurtenances to scientific equipment. Given that clothing and footwear are two very important vehicles for export-led growth (at least in the early stages), the exclusion of SITC 8 should indicate the rate of growth of more capital-intensive imports. Data are provided for imports from the six NICs as well as from a group of ten comprising the NICs and India, Malaysia, the Philippines and Yugoslavia. India and Yugoslavia are major exporters of manufactured goods (although the rate of growth of exports is insufficient for them to quality as NICs), and Malaysia and the Philippines are important members of the second wave of NICs. The growth in importance of the six NICs over the 13-year

TABLE 6.1 Imports from Third World exporters 1968–80,
(measured in one-hundredths of a per cent of GNP in the importing country)

Year	France 6*	France 10*	Japan 6	Japan 10	Sweden 6	Sweden 10	UK 6	UK 10	US 6	US 10	West Germany 6	West Germany 10
1968	0.013	0.040	0.058	0.125	0.145	0.224	0.278	0.300	0.140	0.179	0.092	0.171
1969	0.018	0.056	0.080	0.100	0.177	0.242	0.294	0.399	0.179	0.221	0.120	0.218
1970	0.025	0.057	0.251	0.271	0.171	0.269	0.281	0.372	0.222	0.265	0.157	0.264
1971	0.029	0.061	0.145	0.164	0.159	0.246	0.330	0.419	0.263	0.296	0.155	0.274
1972	0.048	0.094	0.155	0.178	0.200	0.366	0.428	0.477	0.336	0.379	0.197	0.345
1973	0.066	0.124	0.385	0.430	0.260	0.411	0.527	0.675	0.425	0.472	0.250	0.410
1974	0.088	0.155	0.424	0.468	0.296	0.516	0.539	0.659	0.533	0.575	0.296	0.450
1975	0.128	0.181	0.304	0.336	0.332	0.426	0.479	0.588	0.438	0.495	0.344	0.485
1976	0.126	0.198	0.396	0.438	0.416	0.524	0.543	0.708	0.579	0.645	0.450	0.646
1977	0.152	0.235	0.332	0.370	0.511	0.639	0.529	0.709	0.619	0.675	0.444	0.651
1978	0.159	0.231	0.348	0.359	0.409	0.507	0.570	0.744	0.793	0.882	0.443	0.636
1979	0.195	0.276	0.432	0.479	0.477	0.602	0.694	0.861	0.805	0.992	0.531	0.759
1980	0.250	0.342	0.386	0.434	0.512	0.648	0.592	0.723	0.832	0.954	0.568	0.804

* The '6' comprise Brazil, Mexico and the 'four little dragons' (Hong Kong, Korea, Singapore and Taiwan): the '10' include, as well, India, Malaysia, the Philippines and Yugoslavia.

SOURCES: OECD *Statistics of Foreign Trade* and IMF *International Financial Statistics*.

TABLE 6.2 *Manufactured imports from Third World exporters (SITC 8 excluded) 1968–80, (measured in one-hundredths of a per cent of GNP in the importing country)*

Year	France		Japan		Sweden		UK		US		West Germany	
	6*	10*	6	10	6	10	6	10	6	10	6	10
1968	0.009	0.031	0.061	0.111	0.020	0.053	0.074	0.102	0.062	0.093	0.023	0.068
1969	0.011	0.042	0.060	0.078	0.021	0.057	0.095	0.190	0.081	0.115	0.031	0.082
1970	0.016	0.044	0.208	0.226	0.034	0.064	0.099	0.159	0.096	0.131	0.054	0.111
1971	0.017	0.047	0.089	0.106	0.026	0.087	0.116	0.198	0.112	0.138	0.044	0.105
1972	0.026	0.065	0.107	0.121	0.043	0.163	0.145	0.232	0.162	0.195	0.058	0.131
1973	0.036	0.085	0.243	0.278	0.066	0.175	0.218	0.337	0.227	0.262	0.086	0.164
1974	0.048	0.102	0.228	0.275	0.098	0.275	0.223	0.312	0.297	0.317	0.093	0.158
1975	0.048	0.089	0.185	0.214	0.094	0.140	0.172	0.253	0.216	0.252	0.134	0.181
1976	0.067	0.118	0.233	0.268	0.105	0.150	0.181	0.301	0.271	0.309	0.152	0.244
1977	0.071	0.132	0.182	0.215	0.178	0.231	0.173	0.301	0.294	0.327	0.163	0.266
1978	0.085	0.137	0.179	0.205	0.117	0.165	0.237	0.336	0.340	0.448	0.173	0.264
1979	0.103	0.158	0.237	0.272	0.173	0.227	0.285	0.399	0.430	0.490	0.201	0.308
1980	0.139	0.201	0.233	0.269	0.196	0.254	0.234	0.318	0.418	0.507	0.216	0.344

SOURCES: OECD *Statistics of Foreign Trade* and IMF *International Financial Statistics.*

period is evident from the juxtaposing of the two sets of data and by the steady increase in the column pertaining to the 'six' relative the column pertaining to the 'ten'.

The data do not apply to a tranquil world. During the seventies, the industrialised nations introduced their own preference packages under the aegis of the GSP. While most nations instituted their plans in 1972, the US was laggard and did not institute preferential treatment for most members of the Third World until 1976 (Murray, 1977). The UK changed its package of preferences and assumed that of the EEC when it joined the community in 1974. While the effects of the GSP would be to increase the ratio of imports from the Third World to GNP in all the industrialised nations, the packages varied substantially among nations, and the specification of restrictions of varying kinds provided the preference-granting nations with a new and much more sensitive instrument for control over the rate of growth of imports of manufactures from the Third World exporters. In 1976, the EEC signed the Lomé Convention with associated nations (mainly ex colonies located in the Caribbean, Africa and the Pacific), and effectively gave these nations preference over the NICs and other Third World nations. The effect of the Lomé Convention was to divert exports of the associated countries to the EEC and to displace in those markets the exports of the Asian and Latin American NICs and other exporters of manufactures (Tsanacas, 1982). In reaction, these nations focused more heavily on Japan and the US.[9] Since all countries effectively excluded clothing and footwear from the list of goods for which preferences were given, the exclusion of SITC 8 in Table 6.2 can be expected to show greater sensitivity to the introduction of GSP.

The measure of potential adjustment strain is indicated by the absolute increase in the ratio over time. Chart 6.1 shows the data for the 'six' from Table 6.1 in the form of a three-year moving average (limiting the number to eleven). The use of a moving average is designed to smooth out unimportant year-to-year fluctuations. The data show clearly that the US, despite the publicity which has accompanied its institution of orderly marketing arrangements and similar measures, has been subjected to the biggest potential adjustment strain over the 13–year period. Given that the US is the biggest individual market, this must constitute an important contribution to the success of export-led growth. The nation with the smallest potential adjustment strain is France which has consistently positive increments in its ratio, but the increments are very small.

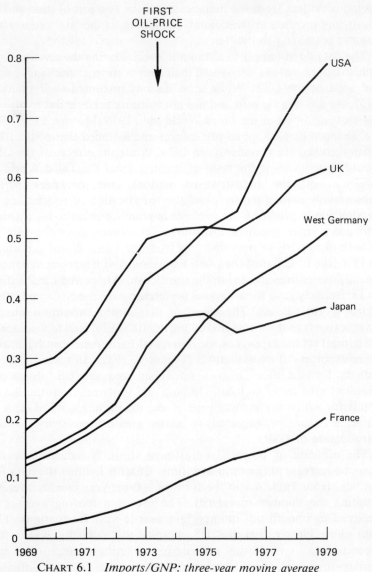

CHART 6.1   *Imports/GNP: three-year moving average*

Note: Swedish ratios have not been drawn: they closely resemble those of West Germany

(France, of all nations, is most likely to be affected by the preferences given to African nations under, first, the Yaounde Agreement and then the Lomé Convention.)

While its interpretation is ambiguous, a more interesting phenomenon is the flattening-out of the ratios of Japan and the UK after 1973. The flattening-out could be attributed to the introduction of the GSP preference package in 1972, and while that would account for the surge in 1973, it is difficult to attribute the very small increases after 1973 wholly to that effect. A second explanation lies in the possibility that both governments, recognising the adjustment strains imposed by the oil price shock (especially for Japan) and internal problems which were coming to a head in the UK, deliberately kept imports of manufactures at a low level in order to devote all their adjustment capacity to the solution of other problems. The data do not prove that either Japan or the UK deliberately set out to slough off imports of manufactures on to other members of the northern bloc, nor that these countries were unsympathetic to the development efforts of exporting nations.[10]

The data do stress the need for some degree of international awareness and cooperation within the northern bloc. It is important to keep protectionist pressure to a minimum if *ad hoc* protectionism is not to blossom at the expense of the viability of export-led growth strategies. The interdependence of markets in industrialised nations must be recognised. It is also very important that the larger markets (the US and West Germany, for example) not be burdened to the point that they ultimately lapse into *ad hoc* protectionism because they reacted more slowly to the imposition of higher costs of adjustment. If, as suggested above, a delayed reaction may be the more violent, the problem of maintaining a global economic climate conducive to export-led development will be seriously aggravated. Export-led growth has been shown to be intrinsically and substantially superior to an import-substitution strategy provided that northern markets are passive: its success requires intra-bloc cooperation in the North. It is also necessary that there be some inter-bloc cooperation. At a minimum, the South must take cognisance of the strains imposed on industrialised countries by their developmental successes. Equally the South must recognise that northern markets cannot be used as a bottomless sink for exports of manufactures from the Third World.

IV POLICY OPTIONS

The magnitude of the problem of large-scale imports of goods using low-skilled labour intensively by northern economies depends directly upon the elasticity of supply of those goods in the southern economies. Here, the combination of a seeking-out of foreign direct investment by many developing nations, and especially of those foreign subsidiaries that are aimed predominantly at supplying northern (and other export) markets, and of large amounts of disciplined, albeit untutored labour at near-subsistence wages, suggests that the elasticity of supply of southern exports is almost infinite in the long run. The establishment of foreign subsidiaries in export zones with their explicit packages of incentives and the willingness of MNCs to transfer technology to cooperative host countries also indicate that the volume of potential exports of manufactures can quickly adapt to any demand which comes from the North. The evidence for a very large long-run elasticity of supply is further reinforced by the efficiency gains which are known to be available to MNCs with production units in the Third World and established marketing and distribution (m&d) organisations in the countries of final use under the same managerial *aegis*. This feature is likely to prove particularly important in facilitating the production of differentiated, experience goods in Third World countries. The pressures to adjust are unlikely to be short-lived as new nations seek to join those achieving development by means of export-led growth. The only reason for expecting that the long-run supply of goods will not grow without virtual limit is the possibility that economies which do not possess Confucian cultures may not have labour forces which lend themselves as easily to training and factory discipline as those of Hong Kong, Korea, Singapore and Taiwan. With the reentry of China into the global economy, there is a plentiful supply of workers with a Confucian attitude. The final reason for supposing that the elasticity of supply of manufactured exports for the South is very high is the potential which exists for MNCs to adapt the Chips-and-Robots technology to southern economies. There are few grounds for optimism that the industrialised economies can escape from the threat of severe cases of accelerated adjustment and of the very high costs of chronic adjustment unless they intervene to reduce the freedom of access of southern countries to northern markets.

This leaves the question as to what type of intervention is likely to prove the least costly in terms of the self-interest of the North and allowing for the role of southern prosperity in that self-interest. As frequently occurs, diagnostic skills exceed the capacity to identify effective, painless remedies. Simple tariffs and quotas have already been considered and seen as potentially unproductive. They merely suppress the disturbance and, at the same time, are likely to result in labour displacement by domestic (northern) industries seeking to reduce their own lack of competitiveness. Even worse, they will prolong into the indefinite future any wage premium which may exist within the protected industry. Even when tied in with conditional protection in the form of a combination of adjustment-retarding and adjustment-effecting measures, they offer little hope of providing the ultimate solution in the absence of accompanying adjustment-facilitating measures. But these measures do not enjoy a peacetime history of effective achievement. Adjustment-facilitating measures may encounter serious problems of institution in democracies if the measures need to subject workers to a discipline which democracies hesitate to impose in peacetime. For example, training (upgrading) programmes might need to separate workers from adverse peer group influence, and this could require geographical relocation in educational work-camps. Even a perfect system of adjustment-facilitating measures becomes ineffectual once the maximum-available supply profile has been achieved and excess supplies of low-skilled workers still exist at subsistence incomes. Subsidy of low-skilled workers seems to be inevitable. Curzon *et al.* (1981) endorse this approach (p. 15):

> A superior approach would be to subsidise unskilled labour and the poorer regions more generally, atlhough it has to be accepted that the results of such policies have been somewhat disappointing in the past. One step towards helping employment of unskilled workers is to reduce the incidence of regressive payroll taxes which are so common in industrialised countries.

Whatever the ultimate degree of success confronting such a policy it is undoubtedly the most effective measure in the short and medium run. There is no need for the incidence of regressivity to be reduced: instead it is possible for payroll taxes to be made (steeply) progressive and this may be the form by which subsidy of low-skilled workers is most effectively achieved. It could also be made to fit in with qualification for retirement incomes. But there is a danger in carrying the details of such schemes too far. The way in which subsidies would be allocated to low-skilled workers is, like all the other revisions to the socio-economic structure which have to be made, particularly sensitive to national culture. Any such arrangements should be arrived at out of a national consensus. What subsidy of low-skilled workers affords is a breathing space in which an economy can learn to cope with the fundamental changes that the two mutually-reinforcing disturbances are inflicting on them.

Subsidy of low-skilled workers will, if effective, reduce the rate of growth of imports from the Southern bloc into the North. The subsidy programme will impede export-led development but this has been seen to be, to some degree, inevitable. It enforces the acknowledged recognition that there exists a practical limit to the rate of growth of southern exports of manufactures to the northern bloc. It is important that the subsidy programme not be limited to tradeable goods, and that it be applied across all industries equally so that actual discrimination against products for the South is reduced to a minimum in terms of the amount of low-skilled labour actually employed. To restrict the subsidy to industries subject to southern competition would be less than a full commitment on the part of the North to minimise the drag its own concerns impose on the process of economic development.

When chronic adjustment costs are inevitable, as seems likely given the mutually-reinforcing quality of the two disturbances, subsidy of low-skilled workers cannot be fully effective. Northern economies will need to institute fundamental revisions of their concepts of economic contribution. (cf. Leontief, 1982). Subsidisation of low-skilled labour buys time for the individual society to evolve in its own way. It is fortunate that both disturbances will contribute to the standards of living available in the North (as well as the South) so that governments may hope to have no one worse off in terms of material well-being.

V   CONCLUSION

The treatment of accelerated adjustment costs in Chapter 4 and of chronic costs in Chapter 5 has led inevitably to a consideration of the policy options. There may be no ultimate solution that can be conceived at this time because of the magnitude of the implications of the changes which are to occur. Societies may have to grope their ways to the ultimate solution as established modes of thought weaken in the face of new realities. Leontief (1982) is recommending that the US begin seriously to contemplate work-sharing but that is unlikely to be a sufficient answer if workers still use a 36-hour week as a reference norm and if they see the marginal revenue from work as exceeding the marginal cost of leisure forgone. Some drastic innovations in systems of taxation may be needed to ensure that workers have no incentive to exceed their allocated hours of work. Excessive hours of work will be rewarded by punitive marginal tax rates determined by wage income measured in hours. (Of course, this situation is likely to put a premium on involvement in the underground economy, but it will also turn workers back to self-sufficiency. The industrialised countries may see rapid growth in the provision of self-service centres for tasks which are normally contracted out at the present time.) Since there may be a severe shortage of very highly-skilled people, the taxation system may need to exempt such people from punitive marginal rates of taxation.

If the world is to find the happy balance between maximum-feasible rates of export-led growth in the South and minimum (tolerable) social costs of adjustment in the North, the realities of the situation must be confronted. Rhetoric ignoring the potential clash of interest is counterproductive. An understanding of the adjustment process becomes mandatory. A maximum effort by the North to develop its socio-economic evolution will be required and pressures on northern economies must be curtailed quickly lest they be temporarily suppressed and emerge later in a more virulent form. Pessimists might argue that the point of no return has already been reached. The resurgence of nationalism and the detestation of imports may already have become excessive and inevitably portend severe (*ad hoc*) protectionism in the future. In that event, a full understanding of the adjustment process may be needed to reverse the protectionist tide and to reestablish a world in which constructive cooperation among the members of the northern bloc, and between North and South, may permit a tolerable compromise.

7 Southern Demands and a Constructive Alternative

Advocates of laissez-faire and free trade have traditionally urged a posture of 'trade not aid' as the keystone of North–South economic relations. Friedman's essay (1958) is the classic statement of this position and derives from what Reder calls the 'Tight Prior Equilibrium' theory, which is the essence of Chicago Economics (1982, p. 11). Built into this set of assumptions is the presumption that income-distributional factors can be neglected in the determination of the efficiency of a policy prescription. This postulate is no different from that which dominates formal welfare economics; such analysis also assumes that the economic system will eventually attain the foreseen long-run equilibrium without any incidental breakdown in the tendency toward equilibrium either cyclically or politically (Gray and Gray, 1982, Section VI). Under extreme conditions, the assumption of stability may not be warranted within a nation and poverty is an essential ingredient in many instances of anarchy and in revolutions. When the component economic units are nation states, the assumption that income-distributional aspects can be safely neglected is tenuous to the point that the postulate becomes misleading in any pragmatic context. None of this means that a 'trade not aid' posture is entirely without merit and needs to be discarded in its entirety. Its contentions that specialisation through market mechanisms will improve the volume of world output (under stationary conditions) and that southern nations might value foreign exchange earned by the surrender of product more highly (and therefore use it more effectively) than foreign exchange transferred as a dole, have a ring of truth. A nation facing competition in its search for needed foreign exchange will be goaded into identifying those products in which its own comparative advantage lies, and export industries will be dragooned by the forces of competition into being as

X-efficient as possible. Put another way, a policy of trade not aid will provide developing economies with many of the incentives needed to ensure that relative prices within their economies do represent actual opportunity costs; this rationalisation has been a major contributing force to the success of export-led growth policies.

Chapter 6 addressed the need for explicit awareness of the existence of political pressures within the North when the pace of adjustment exceeded that compatible with benign adjustment. This chapter is concerned with innate political pressures which exist in the South. The fundamental difference between the two is perhaps that pressures in the North begin at the 'grass roots' or blue-collar level and governments reflect those pressures, while pressures in the South develop at the level of national governments which see extant conditions impeding their success in achieving national developmental targets. In the South, governments and the educated class are those who give rise to the political pressures in the international arena. The cause of governmental dissatisfaction with the extant conditions can be seen as springing from the non-fulfilment of assumptions made in the traditional theory. The South could face, and sees itself facing, a limit to foreign exchange earnings through trade. The traditional theory tacitly assumes that the South has the opportunity to increase its foreign exchange earnings by allowing its (net barter) terms of trade to deteriorate. If northern demand is price-inelastic or political reactions in the North lead to import restrictions being enacted there, then there exists some maximum rate of foreign-exchange earning and the South, as a bloc, faces the possibility of a foreign-exchange constraint on its economic development (McKinnon, 1964). When intra-South competition squeezes out some nations so that a category of least developed nations has to be recognised, then the assumption of stability (and global peace) is endangered.

Section I of this chapter addresses the emergence of the political bloc of developing nations under the auspices of the United Nations Conference on Trade and Development (UNCTAD) in New Delhi in 1968 and the effect of such a bloc on the viability of the free-trade proposals. Section II offers an alternative proposal as a possible means of removing much of the acrimony in the North–South dialogue and so that a constructive base for negotiation can be found. The assumption is that a constructive dialogue is more likely to achieve a viable compromise than a neglect of political realities in both blocs and that the worst of all possible worlds, *ad hoc* protectionism in both blocs, can be avoided.

I   A NEW INTERNATIONAL ECONOMIC ORDER?

The advocates of laissez-faire have never succeeded in installing a complete and exclusive commitment on the part of northern governments to 'trade not aid'. Aid in the form of transfer payments has always been provided to the developing world, both directly and through supranational organisations such as the World Bank. But the flow has never been adequate to ensure a quiescent South. Partly, one suspects, because of their colonial experiences southern nations have always seen the North and the *status quo* as unfairly impeding their economic development potential.[1] This consensus took political shape with the formation of UNCTAD which gave rise to a set of concrete proposals with respect to North–South economic relations (see Kreinin and Finger, 1976). These proposals operate at two levels: on the philosophical plane there is much rhetoric about a pure international economic order or system in which rich countries would not have greater leverage in economic matters than poor countries; on the technical (or economic) plane, the proposals aim at reducing the inequality of economic power by facilitating economic development. The importance of the income-distributional aspects in the eyes of the South can be seen by Patel's summary of the intent of the proposals which constitute the so-called New International Economic Order (NIEO): 'to translate into international economic relations the kinds of objectives and policies which have become the accepted norm within nation states of all modern societies' (1974, p. 3). While Patel did not draw this analogy, his point could be illustrated very aptly with the special treatment, through subsidies of investment, of so-called backward regions in many developed nations (particularly within the EEC).

The NIEO proposals may be seen as attempting to transform conditions in the international economic arena from a set seen as development-retarding to a set which is either neutral or biased in favour of economic development by the South. As in the North (see Chapter 6 above), the rhetoric lacks realism and the South fails to take into account the disruption which their proposals would inflict on northern economies. In consequence, the distance between the two parties is too great for negotiations to bridge.

The idea that the concerns of poorer countries in the global economy merit special consideration was given explicit recognition in the Havana Charter and the proposed International Trade Organisation (ITO) immediately following the Second World War.

The ITO was to form the third leg of a troika of supranational economic bodies (with the International Bank for Reconstruction and Development and the International Monetary Fund). The Havana Charter is interesting because it anticipated the NIEO by almost 20 years. The proposed ITO was to concern itself with the need for economic growth and high levels of employment, with the transfer of economic resources to poor countries, with price-stabilisation schemes for primary products, and with the level of tariffs and other trade-restricting policies. When the overly-optimistic (some would say naive) organisational structure failed to win ratification in the US Senate, the ITO died aborning. One set of its concerns, dealing with trade among developed nations, was transferred to the GATT. Those goals of the ITO which related to the welfare and development of poor nations were forgotten. Had the ITO come into being, it is arguable that UNCTAD would never have been necessary. It is possible that North–South relations might also have evolved more smoothly.

Recognition that the legitimate needs of the developing nations might require more foreign exchange than could realistically be earned (as long as markets in primary products remained reasonably competitive) and that much of the foreign exchange earned was needed for the importation of goods which could not be produced domestically (non-competitive imports), gave rise to a recommendation that aid be institutionalised.[2] Each developed nation was to institute annual transfers to developing nations in the amount of 1 per cent of GNP. This feature of North–South economic relations has never been renounced by either bloc. The concept of the transfer itself presents problems of measurement and definition but these are in the process of resolution. UNCTAD VI in Belgrade in 1983 defined the target in terms of official development assistance thereby excluding items such as the question of military aid (although the line of demarcation can easily be muddied) and any investments made by MNCs. This still leaves difficulties of measurement, particularly the measurement of the aid component of subsidised loans and the treatment of commitments to multinational agencies and to regional development banks.

The transfer of official development assistance is one of the six proposals which constitute the main thrust of the NIEO. Since UNCTAD II in New Delhi, many subsidiary proposals have been added. Official development aid is now agreed to in principle to be set at 0.7 per cent of GNP and that goal is to be attained by 1985; a target of 1 per cent of GNP should be reached as soon as possible thereafter

(UNCTAD Bulletin, 1983).[3]

The other five proposals contain four which have some aid component and a fifth which involves greater facility for exports from the South and, in this way, reinforces the trade-not-aid principle. The four proposals with an aid component are: the SDR link whereby the creation of SDRs by IMF would be channelled through developing nations; the subsidised transfer of technology (Roffe, 1977); stabilisation of primary-product prices by means of a series of price-stabilisation funds to be subscribed by the developed nations; and producers' agreements to increase primary-product prices. While the trade-related proposal is usually couched in terms of preferential access to northern markets for exports of manufactures from the South, it includes the principle that open access to northern markets is essential for economic development.[4] The so-called GSP has already been adopted by developed nations and affords, subject to limitations imposed by (northern) importing countries, preferential access to their markets for the exports of developing nations. The essence of GSP is to allow southern nations to earn foreign exchange by the surrender of goods. It is the sole (major) measure of the NIEO which involves the use of southern resources and which is compatible with the trade-not-aid principle. The proposal was made in 1968 when multilateral negotiations for the reduction of trade barriers were still flush with the success of the Kennedy Round so that the preferential aspect of GSP was always subject to some questions, and it is a moot point whether lower tariffs help or impede southern exports since they lower the degree of preference at the same time as they improve access to those markets for all exporters enjoying most-favoured-nation status.[5] The institution of GSP took place in the seventies when developed nations were beginning to feel the strains of adjustment (as manifested by the adoption of the MFA in 1974). In consequence, the restriction imposed on the categories of goods and the amounts of each good which could be imported under the preferential arrangements were less favourable than had originally been envisaged in New Delhi (Murray, 1977; Rom, 1979; Tsanacas, 1982). One of the most distressing features of GSP was the refusal of the importing nations to include among 'manufactures' goods which transformed agricultural products.

The North–South dialogue underwent a further stage of development in Belgrade in 1983 in UNCTAD VI. This session was dominated by concerns with the then present crisis of worldwide deep recession and the problems of the international financial system deriving from the inability of many debtor nations to service their outstanding international debt, and so the two groups made little tangible progress. For example, Li Ke from the People's Republic of China commented (UNCTAD, 1983, p. 9):

> China was highly dissatisfied with the state of affairs regarding the key issues of the Conference, the resolution of which would be a concrete step toward the establishment of the New International Economic Order. In those areas, developed countries had shown a lack of political will, inflexibility, and a protection of selfish interests.

Because of the absence of China from the world of international economic relations for many years, it is possible that the official Chinese position indicates a simple lack of awareness of the difficulties faced by developed countries and the workings of democracy. It is the rigidities (or economic inflexibility) coupled with the role of the individual which contribute to the North's inability to accommodate the more reasonable demands of the South. What is being argued in this (and the preceding) chapter is that the difficulties extend far beyond 'a protection of selfish interests' in a national or terms-of-trade sense and that recognition of those difficulties by the South is necessary for progress to be made.[6] If the problem confronting the North were a simple question of adjusting to a change in their terms of trade and if the social costs of the adjustment were compatible with not-very-severe costs of an accelerated adjustment, the North's inflexibility and unwillingness to grant the South more open access to its market would be open to severe criticism on moral or ethical grounds.

The key ingredient which is missing in the North's approach is a recognition of the much greater interdependence of the two blocs. The Secretary-General of UNCTAD stressed this new interdependence 'in which the role of the developing countries in the global economy came to be emphasized and underlined in a manner that has been quite unprecedented up to now' (UNCTAD, 1983, p. 9). The weakness lies in the failure of the North to take full cognisance of that fact: 'the recognition of the reality of interdependence was not equally matched by a recognition of its implications'.

The dangers are potentially self-damaging reactions to the sheer inability of the North to effect the measures sought after by the South. Just as the North can generate the worst of all possible worlds (by not recognising the new degree of interdependence) by launching *ad hoc* protectionism, so too the South can become irritated to the point of the institution of socially-detrimental policies. These policies might involve discrimination against developed countries in transactions in which the South would damage itself (and the North) by instituting measures which aggravate the lack of global cooperation. Such measures might include quotas on the use of northern shipping by southern countries; an inimical stance taken toward the location of MNC subsidiaries in southern host countries occasioned by frustration and induced anti-North sentiments (and by their own persuasive rhetoric) rather than by valid economic analysis. Intra-South trading preferences should not be considered counterproductive. Generally, intra-South trading preferences will tend to economise on the use of scarce northern (convertible) currencies and will encourage the manufacture and trade of capital goods in southern economies. The potential problem with such a policy is income-distributional. A country that exports primary commodities to the North could find its pattern of imports diverted by the preference scheme from a relatively efficient northern to a preferred but less-efficient southern supplier. To the extent that intra-South trade preferences could further handicap the economies of the poorer members of the South, some redistribution fund internal to the South might prove necessary.

The South, convinced that the international economic system is development-retarding, has evolved a list of proposals which will improve the possibility of economic development. These proposals have been developed without any reference to their implications for the prosperity of the North (see, particularly, Roffe, 1977, for the more extreme proposals on the ground rules for the transfer of proprietary technology to the South). For want of economic power, the South meets regularly to embroider its proposals and the two blocs meet periodically to discuss the proposals in an adversary setting. The danger is that this situation is likely to deteriorate when the need is for global cooperation. Global economic efficiency will not be enhanced by either bloc instituting myopically self-serving measures which fail to consider the reactions of those measures on members of the other bloc. Just as the North fails to recognise the economic importance of the South, and perhaps because of its fascination with its own rhetoric, it fails to recognise the problems imposed on the South by protection of its own industries. This, of course, does not mean that northern imports of manufactures have not increased substantially (see Table 6.1) but it does mean that that historically-achieved rate of increase will not continue long into the future when the cost of adjustment continues to grow. If the strain in the North–South dialogue increases, it enhances the danger of ever-declining degrees of cooperation in what is essentially a global problem in both its economic and its moral dimensions. The need, then, is for some means of establishing common ground and communication between the two blocs so that one-sided policy actions are not globally counterproductive (reminiscent of the argument for retaliatory optimum tariffs in Scitovsky, 1950).

II A CONSTRUCTIVE ALTERNATIVE

The basic contention of the NIEO that the international economic system, as it exists, is inherently development-retarding rather than development-facilitating is a lineal descendent of the thinking of Raul Prebisch and Hans Singer. If northern markets are not freely open to the point that developing countries' access enables them to earn the amount of foreign exchange that best fits their needs, then some *transfer* of foreign exchange becomes a moral imperative.

What follows is a proposal which is idealistic but which seeks to offer a basis for constructive dialogue and cooperation. It is not and cannot be a complete solution to the problem. It finds its intellectual ancestry in the price stabilisation scheme of the Lomé Convention (Alting von Geusau, 1977). The essential idea is that transfers (or aid) constitute a counterbalance for shortcomings in markets for goods. The Convention provides for the formation of a European Investment Bank and provides a stabilisation fund to compensate the associated members (46 countries in Africa, the Caribbean and the Pacific) in the event of a serious decline in receipts from their principal exports. If these commodities supply more than 7.5 per cent of the country's export earnings, the country becomes entitled to financial help.

If the purpose of any scheme is to create an economic climate which is development-assisting, it must countenance some aid. It must also limit social costs of adjustment to the North to the level which is politically tolerable. The proposal revolves around two meanings of the concept of compensation so that it is useful to specify both meanings of that word quite precisely. In a mechanical sense, compensation means 'to offset a bias or a lack of balance'. In a financial sense, the word implies indemnity or reparation for some obligation.

It is proposed that members of the North set up a Compensation Programme of 20 years' duration. The Programme will have both donor and recipient nations as members. The essence of the alternative proposal is that the North should compensate the South in a mechanical sense for the development-retarding character of the international economic system and in a reparations sense for any measures which individual nation states may take to reduce the severity of their domestic economic problems. Thus, compensation can be defined as *'payment for economic harm experience by a recipient member nation whether or not a donor member is the cause of the harm or merely an actor in a system which is naturally development-retarding at this stage of the evolution of the global economy'*. Compensation is quite distinct from 'foreign aid'. Foreign aid is a transfer payment occasioned by benevolence and/or the hope of the purchase of a political ally. Aid is determined annually by legislatures and aid payments fluctuate from year-to-year according to the caprices of legislatures and international conditions. Aid is discretionary, frequently tied and usually bilateral. In contrast, compensation is largely multilateral and can be distributed in large measure through supranational agencies in amounts predetermined by formula.

The Compensation Programme will consist of a basic 'counterbalancing' transfer payment to the bloc of southern nations plus or minus certain special 'financial compensation' payments. The financial transfer will be added to or subtracted from the basic transfer payments according to the success of the country in export markets. Thus, northern countries choosing to protect sectors of their economies from import competition from the South will increase their contribution to the Compensation Fund. As in the Lomé Convention, transfer payments will be increased when the price of a primary product falls below some pre-agreed norm and a nation's export proceeds from that product fall below some threshold amount. Such payments would be met by an appropriate levy on all donor members according to the value of imports of the commodity in question. Similarly, if the price of a commodity rises above some upper threshold level and revenues exceed some pre-specified amount, a nation's basic transfer receipts will be reduced. Transfers will be made through supranational agencies although this does not preclude a nation making bilateral aid payments up to 50 per cent of its contribution to the Compensation Fund. In the same way, the recipient member will receive less from the multilateral Compensation

Fund. The contributions to and receipts from the Compensation Fund will be computed as 80 per cent of the grant element of the bilateral transfer. Only official development assistance will be counted toward the mandated contribution to the Fund and military hardware and related items will not be included in any bilateral component.

The Fund will receive from each donor nation a basic payment in freely convertible currency equal to 0.6 per cent of the country's GNP. In view of the long-term commitment and the possibility of additional levies and special payments, the NIEO target of 0.7 per cent has been reduced. Donor membership of the Fund will be open to all countries with per-capita GNP in excess of the least rich member of the EEC and will, therefore, be open to oil-exporting nations as well as to the industrialised North.[7] Nations which put limits on imports of products from the South, and discriminatorily or otherwise impede imports from the South shall pay into the Compensation Fund 15 per cent of domestic value added in the protected industry. (This idea is not original here, see Bhagwati, 1977.) Thus if the US, for example, choses to protect its domestic sugar growers (cane and beet) and its shoe industry, it will increase the transfer payments by 15 per cent of value added in those industries. In the first three years of the impediment, the compensation will be paid to member nations which export the impeded goods; for the fourth and fifth years, half the compensation will be paid into the Fund and the other half to exporters of the impeded goods. The principle here is that the most painful effect of protectionism falls not on the established exporters but on countries which are just emerging as significant exporters of particular goods. No distinction is drawn, or need be drawn, between manufacturers, and agricultural goods in this proposal (a very positive feature). Minerals would not be included because their production involves the using up of a natural resource supplied in finite quantity.

Special help will be given to any country whose traditional export fails or falls seriously in price. The criterion here is the same as that of the Lomé of current foreign-exchange earnings. If earnings from that product fall below the pre-determined level from causes other than a reduction in potential supply of an agricultural good or some domestic problem in a mineral, additional payments would be made to those nations to restore their foreign-exchange earnings. If the cause of such a decline were a recession in the industrialised world, the payment would amount to a sort of international fiscal policy and would compensate for the gain achieved by industrialised countries by a decline in the price of a primary product. An agricultural exporter might receive such a payment by virtue of a domestic crop failure due to some natural disaster or because of an excellent harvest in the particular crop worldwide. The kind of negative income-tax payment feature of a recession-induced decrease in price would also describe the payment for an excellent harvest worldwide. The so-called dependency threshold would be agreed to and computed annually as would the expected price. A lower limit of 2.5 per cent of foreign-exchange earnings might be instituted for the least-developed nations.

The plan is symmetrical. The proposal will allow for reductions in the annual amount received from the Compensation Fund by a nation when an important export increases in price and earnings exceed some upper threshold or ceiling. Thus if a nation has a good harvest when other countries experience crop failures or if a nation produces a crop which is a close substitute for one which suffers from a bad crop worldwide, the nation will enjoy very high export earnings and will neither need or receive as much compensation. This aspect of the proposal serves two purposes: it reduces the contributions of the donor members when one or more primary product prices are very high and it introduces a degree of mutual assistance among the members of the South. As in the case of the minimal earnings or dependency threshold, the ceilings will be reviewed annually.

Disbursements from the Compensation Fund will be based on the population of the recipient members at the beginning of the programme (so that no reward will accrue to nations which fail to restrict population growth). The industrialised world cannot be held morally responsible for exorbitant growth rates of population. While it is possible to derive more complex formulae for distribution including one which would allow for greater proportionate payments being made to poor countries, there is much to be said for keeping the basic patterns of operation as simple as possible. This is particularly true in a prototype proposal. Some substantial proportion of the funds would be delivered directly as simple discretionary foreign exchange receipts, although dishonesty by politicians might be kept under control by a system of supervision of the accounts. Another portion of the funds might be used to supply known needs directly. Still another portion of the funds would be disbursed by a development agency according to the value of the project involved; this is essentially the kind of aid offered by the World Bank under International Development Assistance (see Clausen, 1983).

It would become necessary for recipient nations to forfeit membership as their per-capita incomes increased and for their countries to assume a donor membership. The measure for relinquishing membership would be defined in terms of per-capita GDP which would be indexed by some world inflation index. The basic compensation payment would be phased out over a period of five years at a rate of 20 per cent of the original payment per year. When nations relinquished membership, their contributions would be put aside to finance the need for special payments due to decreases in export earnings from particular commodities.

Membership in the Programme will require commitments by both types of members. Donor members would agree to give five years' notice of withdrawal and to contribute their payments during the period of notice. Recipient members would have to obey a code of conduct which would include honouring international debt commitments or making a *bona fide* effort to do so. Subsidiaries of MNCs would, if nationalised, be paid for at some fair rate. Recipient members would be subject to expulsion or suspension for the conduct of military action, irrespective of who instigated the conflict, or failed to live up to a reasonable standard of human rights as laid down in the UN charter. A supervisory board would vote suspension or expulsion, when judgment was involved, by a simple majority. Donor members would also commit themselves to making maximal efforts to increase the adjustment capacity of their economies but the commitment would be underscored by the fact that protection of industries, whether from 'selfish interests' or legitimate concern for the cost of adjustment, would involve an explicit cost in the form of a special contribution to the Compensation Fund.

III   POLITICAL CONSIDERATIONS

The successful negotiation of a Compensation Programme such as that outlined will be fruitless if the Programme is not ratified by the various national legislatures. This section addresses itself briefly to the problem.

In the South, the proposed package could be opposed for internal political reasons as well as for the fact that it fails to provide for specific industries (such as textiles and apparel) and for certain cherished items developed in the original package of NIEO proposals. Its positive points would be the end of the hated concept of 'tying' transferred funds to particular supplier nations and an agreement between North and South which will amount to a good approximation of the basic purpose of the NIEO (cf. Patel,1974). This does not mean that active debate will not take place within the southern bloc but there would probably be a bandwagon effect in that ratification by a critical nucleus of nations would motivate others to follow. There would be great scope for leadership within the southern bloc. There is no need for the full degree of ratification to be instituted at one time; the principle that underlies the most-favoured nation clause might be invoked and then nations could be free to join the programme with all its costs and benefits. Invocation of some sort of most-favoured nation clause would require the exclusion of the nations which abstained from the proposals from other NIEO benefits already in place, and this process could prove very difficult. Alternatively, entry might be open only for certain relatively short periods of time and those nations which did not ratify within the prescribed time period would be required to await a new period of enrolment in the following year.

The problem of ratification in the North would be more severe although some bandwagon effect would probably take place within that bloc simply because of the importance of international prestige. But there are several tangible benefits that would accrue to the North as a result of the Programme.

The major benefit would be the contribution of the Programme to the creation of a stable international economic system for a protracted period. While the Agreement is couched in terms of a 20-year life it is unlikely that relationships would not evolve during that period, but the Agreement would last in virtually unchanged form for several years if only because it would be impossible realistically to assess its effects on the development of members of the South in less than eight years. The existence of a stable international economic system would significantly enhance the prospects for global peace.

Political stability and enhanced rates of growth in southern nations would generate observable economic benefits for the North. The South is important to the prosperity of the North both as a supplier of primary products and as a market for manufactured goods. Greater stability and growth in the South will reduce the likelihood of serious disturbances interrupting the steady flow of a primary product or by the loss of an important market. Some features of the Programme enhance these benefits by increasing the stability of the international system. The reduction of compensation paid to producers of very expensive primary products will reduce the desirability of producers' cartels. The payment of additional compensation, when primary product prices fall excessively as a result of a northern recession, would create a kind of Keynesian contracyclical transfer system whereby the purchasing power of the South would be maintained.

The conditions of membership in the Programme by recipient nations, such as the commitment to shun expropriation of MNC subsidaries without adequate payment in hard currency, will enhance the attractiveness of the Agreement to northern legislatures. The reduction in the number of international negotiations is not to be disregarded. Recently the world has seen a spate of such conferences which cost the taxpayer money, use the time of valuable personnel from all nations and which sometimes seem to aggravate international tension.

Some thorny issues would be eliminated from the world political scene by the adoption of a single 'umbrella' Programme. For example, the thorny problem of the SDR link would be eliminated because funds received by the South under an SDR link would merely reduce the basic contribution to the Fund of the donor nations. This would leave the SDR to be used solely in terms of its contribution to the efficient functioning of the global financial system. Similarly the question of technology transfer will be somewhat reduced since the Compensation Fund proceeds can be used for payments for technology as well as the establishment of research centres in the South.

It is possible that the most important benefit to the North would be the elimination of the existing international economic order as scapegoat for the failure of some southern nations to develop. The Agreement, by effectively eliminating the foreign exchange constraint, places the responsibility for economic development squarely on the shoulders of the politicians and the people in the individual developing nations. Domestic decision-making and policy are fundamental to a good developmental strategy and any system which allows inefficiency to be blamed on outside factors detracts seriously from internal policymaking.

IV CONCLUSION

This chapter, together with Chapter 6, has argued that there is a dangerous lack of communication between the North and the South because neither bloc emphasises the facts which underlie the strain. Chapter 6 argued that the existence of accelerated adjustment costs, particularly when reinforced by the effect of Chips-and-Robots technology, may require some slowing down of the process of change if domestic social costs are to be kept at tolerable levels. The failure to recognise this fact and the conviction that open access to northern markets is a workable ideal has prevented the North from communicating effectively with the South. Similarly the South's unawareness of northern costs, typified by Li Ke's remarks quoted above, as well as a tendency to put its proposals into an extreme form, takes the southern position out of the realm of feasibility. The South is not able freely to communicate its needs in any practical manner. When interdependence is growing, it is dangerous if the parties do not communicate freely and do not mesh their policies at least to the point of avoiding inflicting damage on the other party. This is the danger facing the world at this time. North and South are being drawn closer together by economic realities and by the pattern of evolution of technology and corporate organisation. It is, then, important that politicians become economic statesmen so that this potential conflict can be resolved. A Utopian proposal of a way in which the two blocs might establish communication and confront the problems which face them collectively has been limned in. Given the potential for the Chips-and-Robots technologies to pervade both the North and the South, some accommodation of interest and cooperative adjustment to change is vital to the smooth evolution of the world's economy.

8 Free Trade Among the Industrialised Nations?

The main theme of this book is that there exist sets of conditions under which some departure from free trade may be warranted. The three major reasons for invoking some sort of discrimination against foreign goods are that:

(a) a nation's economy may suffer a temporary loss of competitiveness because of transitory disturbances (frequently in the financial sector). Or an important industry may temporarily lose its international competitiveness but this competitiveness may be regained (to a substantial degree at least) by improving the industry's domestic efficiency. This will take time and conditional protection is warranted to allow the temporary conditions to evanesce or to allow the needed improvement in domestic efficiency to be achieved

(b) the speed of adjustment imposed by the free action of market forces could be excessive and inflict unnecessarily high social costs. Under such conditions protection is warranted to slow down (but not to stop) the process of adjustment

(c) the combination of new labour-saving technologies (chips and robots), together with the enhanced ability of labour-surplus nations to supply manufactured goods which meet the quality requirements of the industrialised world, will create chronic unemployment for low-skilled workers

The role of the developing or middle-income countries in (b) and (c) is evident. For the most part, the arguments for protection deriving from these two mechanisms can be seen in terms of North–South trade, and Chapters 6 and 7 reflect this likelihood. While most of the analysis has been set out in terms of manufactured goods, it could easily be extended to include products with agricultural content involving some product-specific input, and even to services. This chapter considers briefly the possibility that, if political agreement could be reached, the industrial nations would be advised to renounce all impediments to trade within the bloc. For this purpose, the term 'industrial nation' must be more narrowly defined than usual, perhaps to a group comprising Belgium, France, Germany, Japan, the Netherlands, Norway, Sweden, the UK and the US.[1] These are the nations which currently are likely to experience potential labour shortages at cyclical peaks so that supply schedules would quickly become positively-sloped and there would, therefore, be a limit to the amount of damage that one nation could inflict on the others under a regime of binding free trade. The desirability of binding free trade among this group of nations is considered under four separate headings: transitory losses of international competitiveness by a nation or an industry; unequal sharing of the burden of chronic adjustment costs; long-run growth considerations; and a qualification which might provide a workable compromise.

I   TRANSITORY LOSSES OF INTERNATIONAL COMPETITIVENESS

The idea that protection might serve a socially-valuable purpose in the event that an industry (or sector) were to lose its international competitiveness because of some transitory and/or reversible change in conditions in international markets was considered in Chapter 3. While the argument in that chapter did envisage conditions under which protection could be used effectively, the major thrust of the chapter was to strengthen the argument for free trade by curbing the potential costs (domestic inefficiencies) of market imperfections in trading nations. Free trade would also put pressure on X-efficient industries. Temporary protection would be useful in times of self-correcting disturbances, such as temporary currency overvaluation. temporary protection also would 'buy time' or any national industry which had lost its international competitiveness because of a change in the underlying trading conditions, but which could regain the original international competitiveness if given time to improve its domestic efficiency. In such circumstances, conditional protection was considered desirable since it would act as a catalyst for improved domestic efficiency on the part of the threatened (embattled) industry.

A recent issue of concern which might require temporary protection is the concept of 'targeting' which is difficult to define and even more difficult to prove. It has, however, become a matter of sufficient concern that the US Congress gave consideration in 1984 to restricting imports of goods when the home market has been deliberately picked as a target by a foreign industry. The process of targeting involves a deliberate plan on the part of a foreign industry, probably aided and abetted by the foreign government, to establish itself as a dominant factor in the home-country market for a particular good. There are two possible roles for the government: subsidy of industry development and expansion, usually through subsidy of research and development (R & D); and acting as a clearing house for intra-industry cooperation. Presumably two conditions are necessary if a foreign industry is to target a particular foreign industry: it must believe it is capable of acquiring a comparative cost advantage, and the foreign market must be open to imports. Frequently a third condition might be the domestic inefficiency of the home industry. If the home industry is capable of benefiting from the competition and increasing its domestic efficiency so that it can reestablish itself, the problem becomes merely one of an embattled industry. Targeting involves a too-rapid rate of growth of imports, possibly attributable to (foreign) governmental subvention, for the long-run interests of the home economy.

Both conditional protection and simple temporary protection would be lost to industries in industrial nations if an agreement to binding free trade were to be in force. The potential gains of binding free trade in terms of increases in industrial efficiency are almost self-evident. The potential cost might be matter of some concern.

Sectoral or industrial matters are not the only reasons for an unwillingness to renounce the ability to impose temporary protection. Simple reversible disturbances can derive from conditions in financial markets and can be particularly damaging to tradable-goods industries which are exposed to severe foreign competition and whose products are price-sensitive. Such currency misalignments are not unimportant. Kaldor (1971) analysed the effect of currency overvaluation under a regime of adjustable pegs in international financial markets. Currently more important is the possibility that a nation may have a temporarily overvalued currency because of conditions in the capital markets. These conditions prevailed in the US in 1983 and 1984 when the large cash-flow deficit of the federal government forced interest rates to new, very high levels and induced a very large inflow of short-term funds from other developed nations. As if to prove Branson's dictum that, under a system of freely-flexible rates of exchange, the capital account dominates the current account, the strengthened dollar brought about a weakness in the current account of approximately the same amount as the capital inflow (Branson, 1975). It is the temporary quality of the disturbance which damages industries engaged in the production of tradable goods: short-lived capital surges are transitory phenomena which can lead to temporary current overvaluations (even in a world of freely-flexible rates of exchange). Unless prime costs can be reduced to offset the overvaluation of the home-country currency, tradable-goods industries lose market shares and sales volume and both profits and profit-rates suffer. The main damage of currency overvaluation is felt in the loss of dynamism in firms confronting foreign firms in foreign or home markets. Profit-seeking corporations are organic entities and they can be deprived of profits only at some significant cost to their ability to survive in a competitive environment. It is the reduction in profits that constitutes the most serious effect of currency overvaluation.

Firms require infusions of new equipment, new products and new ideas. All the requirements are met out of reinvested profits so that a firm starved of profits becomes less well able to compete. A reduction in the flow of reinvested profit results in reduced expenditures on R & D, product innovation and equipment replacement. The lack of expenditures on R & D, in its broadest sense, together with an inability on the part of the firm to maintain the current quality of its equipment and productive capacity, reduce its ability to compete in international markets in the longer run. At the same time, the firms' foreign competitors are likely to be enjoying above-average profits as higher export prices in domestic currencies combine with increased rates of capacity utilisation and market shares. These foreign firms enjoy a cornucopia of funds which can be devoted to all those activities which are likely to improve the firm's overall competitive position in future years. The damage from currency overvaluation is positively related to the duration of that overvaluation.

A second potentially serious effect of temporary currency overvaluation relates to an asymmetry in the distribution of market shares. It is easier to lose a share of a market than to regain it. Market shares are affected by relative prices and, if currency overvaluation continues for any significant time, the change in relative prices will steadily shift market shares in favour of the corporations benefiting from an undervalued currency. Product- or brand-loyalty will be severely tested and the opportunity is given to foreign firms to create their own degree of product acceptance in what would otherwise be a less accessible group of purchasers. This opportunity coincides with a period when the disparity in internal flows of reinvestment allows the firms with the expanding market shares to exploit this opportunity to the full. Such strategies may include aggressive promotional campaigns, generation of new geographical markets and a strengthening of marketing-and-distribution networks. When the temporary currency overvaluation disappears, the damaged (home country) firms may find themselves with significantly reduced market shares which can only be countered with heavy expenditures on promotional costs. At the same time they need to counter the loss of vitality in product design and manufacturing innovations. Foreign firms may also have access to better managerial talent which may, in the future, affect the X-efficiency of their operations (Leibenstein, 1978).

Firms in industries not exposed to (significant) international competition may suffer the same losses in the modernity of their capital stock and in the vitality of their product design during a period of low profit rates. When the industry again enjoys increased aggregate demand all home-country firms compete on a more or less equal footing, and foreign firms have not had the opportunity to establish themselves in new markets.

Many reversible disturbances would seem to follow from changes in the price and availability of basic materials. For the more narrowly defined group of industrialised countries with a high degree of dependence on foreign supplies of basic commodities, the effect of such a disturbance would be felt more or less equally within the group and should pose no serious problem for binding free trade. Certainly the most obvious example of a temporary loss of international competitiveness – that of the US automotive industry – derived indirectly from a change in tastes consequent, in turn, on a spectacular increase in the price of petroleum. This does not imply that the US automobile industry had not managed to lose so much domestic efficiency, in nearly every dimension of its activities, that it became a prime candidate for targeting. Management was slow to react to new circumstances, labour was overpaid by international standards and the quality (reliability) of the product had decreased steadily.

In a different international setting (such as under binding free trade within the bloc), in which the consequences of domestic inefficiency could be clearly identified in advance, the likelihood of obdurate domestic inefficiencies would be significantly reduced. Economic power blocs would be forced to recognise the implications of any actions on their international competitiveness. Such a world would require a great deal more economic sophistication (and lower expectations about the efficacy of political action) than currently exists. The world has been moving toward a greater recognition of the international dimension and some of the major problems of adjustment in older industries derive from a lack of awareness of the international consequences of past domestic palliatives. If binding free trade within the bloc[2] managed to prevent domestic inefficiencies from arising (as well as imposing possibly harsh cures on existing ones) there would seem to be a strong argument for such an agreement. The gains from the agreement would be likely to overwhelm the social costs of the problems of adjustment. X-efficiency gains would be important, unwarranted wage premiums would be reduced or forestalled and governments would be less willing arbitrarily to handicap (through regulation) tradable-goods industries without gaining agreement on the generality of such measures.

Political agreement would be more easily reached if there were a phase-in period, and a possible escape clause for particular industries or for severe shifts in the terms of trade between primary products and manufactured goods. The problem with all such proposals is that there exist for national governments many non-transparent non-tariff barriers and these then become a means of allowing domestic political pressures to be accommodated.

II UNEQUAL SHARING OF THE BURDEN OF CHRONIC ADJUSTMENT COSTS

The argument presented in Chapter 5 suggested that the combined effects of the huge increase in the capacity for exports of manufactured goods of high standards of sophistication from newly-industrialising countries and their successor nations and of the Chips-and-Robots revolution that is engulfing the global economy in the eighties and nineties will generate permanent unemployment of low-skilled labour in the industrialised nations. These permanent reservoirs of unemployed workers are the chronic adjustment costs. As a counter to the international dimension of the problem, some means of curtailing imports of manufactures into the industrialised bloc (particularly of goods which used low-skilled labour intensively) would be instituted along with a compensation scheme to compensate the frustrated exporters. The major impact of the problem would be felt in rich countries (including the narrowly-defined industrialised countries) and changes in social contracts would be needed in many nations to accommodate the possibility that large numbers of people might spend their lifetime without gainful employment. Any financial cost of accommodation would be met by the central government and have implications for the levels of taxation within the industrialised bloc. But the problem has its domestic causes as well, and a cunning industrial nation could reduce its own costs of chronic adjustment problems by running an intra-bloc surplus on those goods which use labour intensively.

Such a scheme would involve the covert (non-transparent) subsidisation of goods using large amounts of (unskilled or low-skilled) labour so that the nation would assume the position of prime supplier of such goods within the industrial bloc. Flexible exchange rates and similar propensities to save out of private-sector income would enforce balanced current account (in the absence of continuing capital flows). Subsidisation of the factor in chronic excess supply would enhance the demand for that factor within the country but not within the bloc and that country's costs of chronic adjustment would be successfully shifted on to other members of the bloc and thereby reduced, the surplus on labour-intensive goods being matched by an intra-bloc deficit on high-technology goods.

Concerns about the possibility of such behaviour would make successful negotiation of binding free trade very difficult indeed. The contingency would have to be allowed for in the agreement and some punishment for non-compliance defined. The existence of chronic adjustment costs would be likely to require a completely new approach to the question of free trade because of the continuous temptation to protect home industries for the purpose of enhancing employment. A new form of mercantilism would begin to emerge. The traditional context of potential full employment would not be relevant and international economic cooperation would become increasingly difficult to arrange and to preserve.

III LONG-RUN GROWTH CONSIDERATIONS

The doctine of free trade, unless qualified by modified free trade and modified laissez-faire, rests explicitly on the absolute efficiency of the unrestrained operation of the market mechanism as a means of generating global income and wealth. The income-distributional aspects of the doctrine are less convincing. In principle, it is possible for workers to earn less than welfare-subsistence income even when fully employed. When the income-distributional implications of free trade drastically change the relative levels of income between nations, then the frustrations with a simple laissez-faire solution grow dramatically. Then nationalism and self-interest can combine into a powerful force working against the free-trade solution.

If the income-distributional aspects of the free-trade model are moot, so too are its implications for economic growth, and the distribution of such growth among nations. There is an underlying presumption in all the arguments for free trade that the absence of artificial impediments to international trade will speed up economic growth worldwide. Higher global incomes will lead to larger flows of saving and investment (if not higher rates) and growth will be accelerated. The distribution of that growth among nations will lead to faster rates of growth in countries with high propensities to save (unless such saving is siphoned off through international capital flows). If free trade affects the level of income of a country unfavourably, it will almost inevitably have an adverse effect upon the rate of growth of income. The second dimension whereby free trade will help in the growth process is by enforcing change. Walter (1981–2, p. 18) points out the value of international trade and competition in 'weeding out' decaying domestic sectors of the economy: 'anything that interferes with this constant "churning" between healthy and unhealthy sectors of the national economies necessarily retards growth. Clearly, barriers thrown up against import competition have this effect.'

In the terms developed in Chapter 4, Walter is assuming a global pull adjustment process. The infant-industry argument for protection is the only one which traces its rationale directly to concern with economic growth. In practice the concern is more with economic development than with simple economic growth, and the argument rests on the ultimate comparative advantage of an industry which cannot be established in a country because of a lack of cost-competitiveness in its infancy. The lack of competitiveness may derive from the lack of workers with the appropriate industry-specific skills in the domestic economy, the lack of experience in the industry and the absence of suitable local ancillary production units and the existence of substantial scale economies in foreign productions units. Many economists, particularly those advocating export-led development, and those who subscribe to the free–trade doctrine without reservation, oppose infant-industry protection on the grounds that it impedes rather than enhances economic growth. Two major lines of attack are common. Many so-called infant industries have not achieved the cost reductions over time that were expected of them. They have tended to become domestically inefficient instead of steadily reducing their comparative cost disadvantage against imports as total production increases. In addition, any positive growth impetus given to the infant in duty has the disadvantage of penalising downstream industries by forcing them to take output at costs higher than could be obtained from abroad, and in this way making the downstream industries more vulnerable to foreign competition.

A variation of the infant industry argument involves the erection of protective devices against imports as an inducement for technology-rich foreign MNCs to establish production subsidiaries in a developing country (Gray and Walter, 1983). Here the relationship between growth and protection hinges on the efficiency of so-called spread effects (Myrdal, 1957, p. 31) whereby the ambient economy gains in efficiency and knowhow as product and process technology seep out of the MNC subsidiary. This spreading of technological knowhow comes about as workers in the subsidiary inculcate the skill learned on the job into their local cultures, or as local firms become suppliers to the subsidiary and are 'trained up' to work with new machines and to produce output with closer tolerances.

The final possible relationship between economic growth and free trade has overtones of the spread-effects mechanism, and is of particular importance to the focus of this chapter since it has recently been identified and acted on by France. French international economic policies have always been marked by an alive awareness of the benefits for the French economy, and by a haughty disregard for the high-flown and impractical theories of abstract economics. If the French choose to disdain the lessons of high theory, their past record entitles their action to a respectful analysis based on realities rather than on arrantly abstract assumptions. For simplicity of exposition only, this argument for growth-inducing protection is set out in terms of a home country (France) and a foreign country (Japan). The essence of the argument is that even a modern industrialised country cannot afford to have a major piece of modern technology remain alien to its economy and enjoyed only through imported goods which embody it.

Consider a piece of proprietary technology developed by a Japanese firm of the kind that is so basic and so potentially important that it will give rise to the kind of industry technology cycle described by Magee (1977). An industry technology cycle exists when the number of inventions and innovations which take place within an industry increase with the age of the industry for a period of time and generate an S-curve relating the number of industry patents (on the vertical axis) and the age of the industry (on the horizontal axis). According to Magee (1977, pp. 305–6):

> The steeply rising part of the curve suggests that a major breakthrough may have occurred in one product in the industry which stimulates the demand for new components. The new information implicit in the development of a major new product will have complementary applicability to other products in the same industry. At any point in time, we know that the marginal returns on additional information, just like the marginal returns on any other input, will fall until (the present value) of the marginal revenue product of the last unit of information just equals the cost of that information. This applies to *flows* of information in the short run.

While Magee stresses the intra-firm dimension of the process, it is legitimate to stress the potential for developing complementarities of information within an economy. The new technology, X_1, makes possible a new product and has the prospect of correlating with other knowledge (existing and concurrent) to develop a series of derivative technologies which will enhance economic growth rates into the foreseeable future. These derivative pieces of technology can be called X_{2i}, X_{3j}, and so on, where the numbered subscript denotes the generation of the derivative technology in terms of the basic invention, 1, and i and j indicate the number of pieces of parallel technology in each generation. It may be assumed that $j > i > 1$. France has access to X_1 by importing it embodied in tangible goods, by having the Japanese proprietor license the technology to a French firm, or by having the Japanese firm establish a subsidiary in France using the technology (and obeying French requirements about the indigenisation of managerial and R & D personnel). Given the inefficiences of the market mechanism for the transfer of proprietary technology, the second adoption is not encouraging, and unless the French economy has any natural or comparative advantage in the manufacture of goods embodying X_1 once the technology is made available there, the Japanese firm would be unlikely spontaneously to establish a production subsidiary in France and would choose to supply the French market by exporting from Japan or from some newly-industrialising area. Consider now the possibility that the probability that French nationals (firms or individuals) will manage to share in the development and ownership of some of the X_{2i} or the X_{3j}, say, is positively related to the use of X_l in France. Future French economic growth will be adversely affected by free trade since the opportunity for French firms to benefit from the ownership and employment of the derivative technologies is reduced if the goods are imported.

Long-run growth considerations can therefore offer a reason for protection against the importation of technological non-competitive goods (Gray, 1976a, p. 47). As noted, France, with its great pragmatism, has recognised this and encouraged the production of computers in France by implying that government-sector purchase might discriminate in favour of firms with physical production on French soil.[3] Given the size of the government sector in France and despite the agreements made during the Tokyo Round, this is no empty gesture. In a less important but more spectacular action, the French Government imposed highly artificial restrictive barriers to the importation of video cassette recorders from Japan. These goods were to clear customs only in a very small office in Poitiers, where a small number of inspectors imposed minute inspection procedures on each unit (Dionne, 1983).[4] When an agreement had been reached for the product to be made locally, the obstructionist measures were removed.

The argument for protection as a potential stimulus to economic growth has been imputed to the French. The argument that no economy can afford to be deprived of the use of important new technologies within its borders makes good intuitive sense. The kind of reasoning which seems to underlie the practicality of past French economic policies is quite consonant with the imputation. Certainly economists cannot refute the argument. The free-trade doctrine relies on an essentially static or comparative static frame of analysis so that the problem exceeds anything which trade theory is capable of solving. Nor have growth theorists sufficiently incorporated the process of intergenerational technological development to such a degree of refinement as would permit formal analysis of the relative costs of protection and deprivation of basic technology.

Concern with long-run effects of reliance on technological non-competitive goods could be a very severe political obstacle to the creation of a binding free-trade agreement among the industrialised nations. Problems of access to new technologies could be circumvented by some complicated arrangement specifying conditions under which licensing would automatically be made available. Such a degree of international economic cooperation is rather more than modern economists have any valid reason to expect, particularly under conditions of severe, if not chronic, adjustment costs. This possibility of a perceived need for the local use of a potentially valuable piece of technology will reduce the likelihood that binding free trade could be negotiated within the industrialised bloc or that, when negotiated, the arrangements would not be violated by covert measures.

IV   A VARIANT ON BINDING FREE TRADE

The benefits of binding free trade among the industrialised nations in economic terms are self-evident, particularly if existing situations are given some period of adjustment. In the absence of rapid changes in trade patterns within the bloc, free trade would promote domestic efficiency as well as allocating production internationally according to relative opportunity costs. Yet, nations and their politicians would be hesitant to agree to binding free trade in any absolute sense because changes in underlying conditions could provide valid arguments for short-term protection as well as exciting domestic political pressures for such protection. Binding free trade would preclude many of the options currently available to politicians.

The main consideration among the industrialised bloc as well as in terms of North–South trade (chronic adjustment costs possibly excepted) is the rate of growth of imports (that is, the rate of imposed adjustment). It may be possible to include in a programme of binding free trade a temporary outlet which would provide for short-run relief; the programme might be called 'modified binding free trade'. The industrial nations would agree to institute free trade with each other on the sole condition that each nation would have the authority to restrict the growth of imports of any individual good to 5 per cent per annum by number or by value. This condition would be reminiscent of the 'escape clause' of the GATT (Clause XIX) except that it would be capable of being imposed even when no reduction in obstacles to trade had been invoked. The measure could be imposed unilaterally and *sine die*.

There are several arguments in favour of 'modified binding free trade'. The first two are essentially pragmatic: the concept is simple; and a free-trade agreement is more likely to be reached with such a condition than without it. It would be necessary to reach a consensus among the members of the bloc with respect to the definitions of the categories of goods and services to which the 5 per cent clause could be applied and there would be obvious difficulties in determining the limit in terms of units when the agreed-upon category was a composite. The economic benefits of the 5 per cent clause could be significant since the clause addresses directly the basic disruptive influence which free trade can impose on an economy: speed of adjustment. At the same time, the clause does preclude arrangements whereby imports are capped or allowed to increase far more slowly than is desirable from an efficiency standpoint. A rate of growth of imports of an individual category of good would permit substantial growth in the absolute volume of imports over a protracted period despite the imposition of the clause. At the same time, the clause allows a legitimate 'breathing space' for any industry which needs time to adjust or for any problems of labour market congestion. A 5 per cent growth rate will double the absolute volume or value of imports in just over 14 years and the home industry is faced with inexorable pressures for its ultimate elimination at the same time that politicians enjoy a ready-made answer to pressure.

The value would need to be measured in some international numeraire and indexed in periods of rapid inflation. It would also be desirable to have the permitted quantity of imports computed in terms of the (recent) previous highest quantity of imports so that recessions would not adversely affect the growth of imports. The concept of 'modified binding free trade' would not need to be subscribed to by everyone at the same time. The agreement could be reached by those countries farsighted enough to adopt the proposal and other nations could be admitted when they were willing to join. The proposal could spread in the way that most-favoured nation treatment expanded during the nineteenth century. The proposal has the possible disadvantage that it might seriously weaken such existing arrangements as the EEC.

V CONCLUSION

There are two very large gains to be achieved from the establishment of binding free trade among the industrialised nations. To facilitate the cost of adjustment, it might be desirable to introduce a safety valve in the form of a 5 per cent clause which restricts the possible rate of growth of imports and which can be imposed unilaterally by any member nation on all its trading partners. The safety valve would ease the problems that accompany transitory losses of competitiveness, of attempts to slough off a part of the burdens of chronic adjustment and, by limiting the rate of increase of imports of new products with important technological content, could encourage local manufacture.

9 Summary and Conclusions

Indeed, it is a widely held view in Japan and Western Europe that the 1980s will be a difficult decade of major structural adjustment, with extraordinarily high levels of unemployment to be expected. This transformation will be, in their eyes, driven by the emergence of new competitors from the developing world, by the emergence of Japan as a major competitor in the frontiers of technology, and by technology itself. These governments therefore feel that they must guide the inevitable structural transformation, and mitigate its potential for social and economic disruption to jobs, key sectors and key regions. (Malmgren, 1983, p. 200).

The question which this book has posed and attempted to answer is 'How best can the guidance of the inevitable structural transformation be accomplished?' International trade theory has neglected analysis of the problems inherent in the reallocation of resources among sectors and has traditionally assumed that the market mechanism will work to accomplish the necessary adjustment in an efficient (least social cost) manner. This neglect of adjustment underlies the unswerving devotion of many economists to the first-best solution of multilateral free trade. This devotion to unimpeded international trade (and investment) characterises the philosophy of the Reagan Administration in the US and will present a source of international economic friction between Europe and the US. In a world of docile economic factors, strong competitive forces, small and infrequent shocks and benign adjustment there is a very strong case to be made for the policy of multilateral free trade. National defence (a grievously overworked excuse) and protection of key industries by developing countries without fear of retaliation are probably the only two exceptions which would command general agreement.

This book has presented the argument that a simple reliance upon a hands-off attitude to problems of economic adjustment can be ill-advised and that, under turbulent conditions, protective measures have a role to play in interventionist adjustment policies. A complete reliance on the efficacy of the market mechanism in a decentralised economy is not unique to considerations of adjustment following new conditions in the supply and demand for goods. Balance-of-payments theory has an equal faith in the unaided workings of the market mechanism or, which amounts to the same thing, an equally fearful reluctance to prescribe (or even to consider) government intervention in the inter-sectoral adjustment process. The absorption theory considers a change in relative prices of home and foreign goods (an expenditure switch), coupled with measures to ensure that needed availability of resources (an expenditure reduction) an adequate explanation of balance-of-payments adjustment. In this literature, the imposition of a tariff is seen as one possible means of effecting an expenditure switch (and therefore changes in resource allocation) but currency depreciation is perceived as the main and most efficient instrument variable. The *modus operandi* of depreciation is a straightforward neoclassical mechanism of the operation of market forces under competitive conditions so that the pressures to adjust are inexorable and, it must be assumed, adjustment takes place without introducing a financial collapse or depression as a balance of payments is attained before the deficit nation runs out of international reserves. The failure of balance-of-payments theory to consider possible weaknesses in the adjustment mechanism (other than the Marshall–Lerner criterion) and the possibility that the authorities might usefully intervene in the adjustment process, may help to explain some of the apparent difficulties in eliminating balance-of-payments deficits.

This passive reliance on the efficacy of the market mechanism, when aided by the appropriate set of macropolicies, is reflected again in a debate on the virtues of 'industrial policy' in the US in the mid-eighties. Schultze (1983) argues against the use of industrial policies which he defines as a combination of 'protecting the losers' (by commercial policies and similar adjustment-suppressing measures) and 'picking the winners' which entails identifying growth industries and supporting them through government assistance (including subsidisation, promoting intra-industry joint R & D and similar measures). The problem which industrial policy addresses resembles that of adjustment but is not identical. Schultze sees industrial policies as a set of micro-level interventions by the US government aimed at adapting the US economy to new global conditions and technologies and at preventing an erosion of the share of GNP attributable to manufacturing. The essence of Schultze's argument is that the authorities should not intervene at the micro level to facilitate the transfer of resources among sectors because they are not competent to do so: government is not capable of picking the winners and actions taken to protect the losers are seen only as adjustment-suppressing measures and not as positive policies. This argument bespeaks a passivity of outlook which is somewhat at odds with Schultze's willingness to intervene actively to generate a fitting macroeconomic environment by traditional Keynesian methods.

The question at issue may be one of the degree of precision of the policies under consideration. Tinbergen (1970, p. 2) distinguishes between quantitative and qualitative policies. Quantitative policies are those made in an unchanging economic structure, i.e. the set of structural equations and the coefficients of the individual variables in those equations do not change either because of the policy adopted or because of changes in the underlying conditions. Qualitative policies are those which respond to a new matrix of coefficients in the structural equations induced by changes in the underlying conditions or which alter the matrix of coefficients by changing the interrelationships. Manifestly, policy intervention to aid the need for adjustment must involve qualitative measures. Tinbergen is not optimistic with respect to the success of the implementation of such measures because 'our empirical quantitative knowledge of human behaviour under different structural conditions is so restricted' and he concludes that 'the scientific treatment of problems of qualitative policy meets with great difficulties' (1970, pp. 68–73). It seems likely that both Tinbergen and Schultze have a much more precise concept of policy formulation and intervention than problems of adjustment allow. They seem to seek the same precision that is implicit in Tinbergen's models in which the main sources of errors are minor inaccuracies in data. In a turbulent world, even quantitative policies lose their precision. So-called fine-tuning has proven an abject failure in purely quantitative policies as soon as western European countries and the US lapsed from a world of tolerable tranquillity and with the end of the willingness of the major nations (including the US) to allow the US to play the passive role of the nth country in the international financial system. There must be a discomfiting aura of imprecision in any interventionist policy which responds to or countenances structural change. Imprecision is a necessary ingredient of adjustment policy. But the exactness of quantitative policy is superficial, if not spurious. Both macroeconomic policy and adjustment policy will call for a groping process whereby the target is approached by increments. Given the uncertainty which prevails, especially in the knowledge of the effectiveness of certain policy instruments, policy must become more tentative as the target is approached. The greater the uncertainty the less precise is the policy process.

Policy makers have good knowledge of the actual position and must have reliable knowledge of the direction of change required to move towards the new target. The greater the 'distance' between actuality and target, the less necessary is it for policy makers to have precise knowledge of the characteristics of the target state in order to feel confident about the required direction of change. Schultze identifies many areas in the US economy in which the incompatibility between reality and the post-adjustment economy is so stark that the direction of change can be identified with confidence (1983, pp. 13–14) and in which intervention would be beneficial. In this sense, Schultze seems to admit to the possibility of adjustment policy while arguing against industrial policy. Similarly Schultze admits the potential benefit to be derived from the institution of adjustment-facilitating measures. He does not conceive of adjustment-effecting measures perhaps because he has too little faith in the political system to impose conditional assistance and to terminate that assistance if the conditions are not met.[1]

The argument for interventionist adjustment policies would seem to depend upon the distance or disparity between reality and the post-adjustment target.[2] If the disturbance is a trend disturbance and will increase with the passage of time, then adjustment policy is more likely to prove valuable. As the distance decreases, interventionist adjustment policies become more tentative. The purpose of adjustment policy is to assist the market mechanism, not to supplant it as it gropes toward the target situation. It is when the distance is large, or growing faster than market forces alone can correct, that commercial policy measures along with other policy interventions can be invoked as a legitimate policy option.

Michalski (1983) suggests that the appropriate target during the process of adjustment is that mix of output which allows the economy to generate high rates of saving and the ability of the economy to cope with shocks benignly. All analyses of adjustment policies have stressed the need for high levels of employment (to avoid the broad version of labour-market congestion).[3] Unfortunately, if the disparity between actual and target is severe, the effectiveness of traditional macroeconomic policies may be reduced and there will be no assurance that standard macropolicies can generate anything close to full employment.

The likelihood that the disparity between actual and target will attain the magnitude needed for interventionist adjustment policies to be instituted is greatest when disturbances are large and/or severe and when successive disturbances are mutually-reinforcing or cumulative and follow hard on one another. Note that the decision to release a suppressed disequilibrium will itself constitute a shock: the longer the disequilibrium has been suppressed if the disturbance is a trend disturbance, the more the original dislocation will have magnified itself with the passage of time and the greater will the actual shock be. Such events frequently occur when governments change or when a set of economic institutions that has outlived its usefulness, has, with all the tenacity of a retiring opera or film star, hung on for longer than is beneficial and is finally disbanded. The fixed rate of exchange of the US dollar under the Bretton Woods system was such an event but it was promptly overshadowed by the first oil-price shock.

The argument of this book is that the opinions attributed to Japan and western Europe by Malmgren (cited at the beginning of this chapter) will prove valid. Moreover the transformations required will be made much more difficult and socially costly by the fact that the workers who prove to be surplus in the short run (at least) will be predominantly workers with low levels of transferable skills. Thus in addition to what might be termed straightforward adjustment in which displaced workers need retraining in other industries at previously-attained skill levels, the transformation which is likely to occupy the eighties and beyond will require that workers be upgraded in terms of their skill levels. The amount of upgrading required may be substantial. The pressures created by shocks which have already taken place have used up the latent capacity for (easy or straightforward) adjustment in the industrialised countries and have generated a surge of protectionist fervour and protectionist measures. Not only are these problems likely to be difficult to solve but, by inflicting the brunt of the social cost on low-skilled workers in the industrialised nations, the shocks pose a serious moral problem as well. In many industrial nations, the costs of protracted unemployment can be severe (Brenner, 1976, Marshall, 1983). If the disturbances are so severe and so large that adjustment costs become chronic rather than simply accelerated, then even more far-reaching changes in national economic and social structures will be required.

Such measures will transcend the boundaries of economics as narrowly and traditionally defined and analysts will be required to broaden their areas of concern. The moral aspects of the problem also have repercussions which will adversely affect the Third World. This is inevitable when the major disturbance is likely to be labour-saving technology rather than changes in international trade patterns and when the major resource of Third World nations is labour. Analysis of the problem cannot be limited to the industrialised countries. Some thought must be given to bridging the gaps between the two blocs and to ensuring that any adverse repercussions in the South from measures adopted by the North are kept to a minimum. Failing that, the world runs the risk of much higher levels of international tension than might be achieved with widespread prosperity. The argument for adjustment policy resembles that put forward by Walter (1983, pp. 515–16) for the world steel industry: the problems must be confronted with a view to minimising the severity of their impact, that is, 'damage control'.

The theory of international trade effectively assumes away costs of adjustment and is suitable for an era of slow evolutionary change rather than for a turbulent time of large and severe trend disturbances. Current actuality seems to be a helter-skelter series of transfers of technology to labour-surplus nations, rapid industrialisation, trade-facilitating new commercial linkages, and a rapid pace of technological evolution in the industrialised world. In the modern world some understanding of adjustment policy and its limitations will be required and some of the old dicta will have to be discarded. Among the latter is the impossible dream of a liberal (or free) trading system operating smoothly under the GATT. Political forces in the industrialised nations are violating such a system. This new state of affairs puts heavy responsibilities on both theorists and participants. Theorists must address the working of the economic system under stress of adjustment pressures. There is a danger that continued emphasis on simplified models of the world in which a first-best solution is believed to be attainable may inflict greater social costs than could be achieved by sensible but restrained interventionist adjustment policies. This will require profound reeducation of politicians who have been educated by generations of economists in the advantages of free trade in a static world. The burden placed on politicians and policy makers is even heavier. Politicians must engender adjustment-facilitating measures even though their apparent efficiency will not be immediately apparent nor easily measured. Politicians must have the courage to institute adjustment-effecting measures including phase-out protection and the removal of quasi-rents in declining industries. The pre-eminent virtue of free trade is that it allows the market mechanism to work inexorably and the market will not suppress a disequilibrium (however tempting that may be to a politician). But the market will, almost inevitably, impose very (and unnecessarily) high social costs, particularly in old countries with sectoral rigidities and low saving-rates.

The whole process of adjustment centres around factor markets. Commercial policy is directed at product markets. Commercial policy may need to be transmuted or qualified in some way if it is to be used as an ingredient in adjustment policy: maintaining demand for a domestic import substitute will not be productive if resources are attracted into the industry or if the surplus factor is displaced by another factor of production.

The political docility of factors in different countries and of countries themselves has been much reduced in recent years as expectations about the ability of governments and world bodies to influence economic activity have risen. People seem to have come to believe that a clever government can control the world's economy and their own economy in particular and to control it so that it yields steadily high levels of employment and steady increases in average income. In turbulent years, these expectations cannot but be disappointed. Such disappointments will not make the task of instituting sensible adjustment policies any easier.

Appendix A: Canterbery's Vita Theory of Income Distribution

The main thrust of a vita theory can be simply stated. Assume that one labour market exists for each general human capital classification. The individual's quantity of human capital determines *which* labour market the person enters. A person 'qualifies' for a particular labour market by the state of his or her vita at that point in time. Determination of vita begins at birth when one's race, sex, religion, national origin, inherent mental and physical capacity, inheritances, and family background are duly noted. (Canterbery, 1979, p. 12)

Canterbery's integration of human capital and labour market theory has provided a rich analytic framework with which the adaptation of the supply of labour by skill and skill level to changes in demand can be examined. In a book devoted to the analysis of the adjustment mechanism and the virtues of a simple 'laisser-passer' policy in facilitating that mechanism, the vita theory is vital. Simple neoclassical, homogeneous labour markets are not enough to allow identification of the costs. This appendix summarises the vita theory insofar as it is directly applicable to the process of adjustment. No suggestion is made that this brief treatment captures the full richness of Canterbery's analytic insights.

Let there be n categories of general human capital. These may be ranked by the inherent skill level although the ranking process may be difficult in any comparison of the skill levels of highly-trained specialists in different professions. Within each general category, there exists a number of 'occupations' or sub-specialities. The separation of individual tasks into occupations depends upon the elasticity of substitution in supply. Let the category of general human capital with the most occupations – probably the category of unskilled labour – have m occupations. There exists an n by m matrix of specific human capital with a large number of zero elements. Each cell of this matrix contains the number of persons who are qualified, by their vita, to perform the task in question. Because the wage will be positively related to the level of human capital involved, each person will place himself or herself in the highest cell attainable. Within each cell, people will be ranked according to the quality of their vita relative to the others in the cell. Such a matrix can characterise a labour force by the distribution of the work force in the various cells. There will exist a matrix of this kind for each geographical area within the national labour market. The regional or geographical submarket is identified because it is impossible for a worker to relocate spatially in the short run. There exists a comparable matrix for the demand for labour. Within each cell is given the number of workers required. Within each region, firms will have capital equipment in place and the combination of the features of the stock of capital equipment, the level of total demand for goods and services and the mix of that demand will determine the short-run demand for labour.

Both matrices exist at a point in time. By subtracting the number of workers in the cells in the supply matrix from the number in the equivalent cell in the demand matrix, a matrix of excess demand can be developed. Where excess supply exists, the unemployed will consist of those workers with the lowest ranking vitae within the cell. It is unlikely that there will ever be a perfect match (except in some elusive steady state) because both matrices will evolve over time. Evolution in the demand matrix will be generated by changes in the level and mix of goods demanded, by spontaneous changes in technology and by induced changes in the labour-intensity and skill-intensity of the capital stock in response to varying patterns of relative wage-rates. Evolutions in the supply matrix may be expected to be almost wholly induced as people respond to the pattern of excess demand for labour and to any anticipated changes over the foreseeable future. Evolutions in the supply matrix can also result from changes in the efficiency of educational institutions.

An individual acquires a vita over time. The details determined by birth – the birth vita – are extremely important and determine genetic traits – mental and physical – and the family environment which may assist or discourage the acquisition of human capital through attitude or the availability of assets. On the basis of the pre-career experience, the vita evolves and reflects the various kinds and intensities of education and training received. Finally, a worker has a 'mature vita' which describes the quantity and quality of training, education and experience. Familial environment and genetic endowments affect the mature vita through the ability of the person to obtain and absorb training. It is these vitae which determine the ranking of individuals within the cells of the supply matrix. A worker will attempt to maximise lifetime income by acquiring human capital, at the expense of leisure and other assets, until the expected return to additional human capital is equal to its cost. In this search, the individual is constrained by the availability of nonhuman assets (with which to finance additional education and training) and by the birth vita. If best use has not been made of mandatory schooling, the individual is also constrained by factors contained in the pre-career vita.

Mobility among markets is limited. In the short run, a worker cannot move from one market to another. In the long run, a worker may move spatially (from one regional submarket to another) or may downgrade himself or herself to a lower category of general human capital. In the very long run, a worker can acquire additional human capital and upgrade himself or herself. Downgrading involves a loss of caste and is not lightly undertaken. A worker who has downgraded himself or herself is considered to be underemployed in terms of the human capital available. The temptation is always for younger workers, who are likely to be the least qualified within a cell, to downgrade themselves. In times of recession or depression, widespread downgrading may occur and a downgraded worker may be expected to be ranked very highly in the new cell and may displace a worker already employed. This process can lead to bumping so that the lowest level of general human capital will tend to have a disproportionate share of total unemployment.

In addition to the difficulties in adjustment described in the preceding paragraph, there exist 'artificial' impediments to movement caused by licensing requirements and craft and industrial unions' restrictions on entry into a cell.

Structural unemployment exists when the demand and supply matrices do not correspond even when the capital stock is being fully utilised. Structural unemployment, then, results from a mismatch between the skill-mix demanded by employers and the skill-mix available from the work force. When structural unemployment exists, the supply matrix can adjust as workers relocate geographically, as workers acquire additional human capital or retool to acquire specific skills which lie within their capabilities, or downgrade themselves to cells in which excess demand exists. Bumping may also be a feature of structural unemployment but it is also associated with unemployment due to inadequate aggregate demand. With the exception of bumping, all the adjustments are likely to be more easily accomplished by workers in the higher categories of general human capital. The acquisition of additional human capital implies the availability of financial resources. The acquisition of new specific skills implies a switch among closely-related professions. The ability to relocate geographically is also related to high levels of human capital because of the better informational networks available at high levels of human capital and the ability of high-level workers to fund the costs of relocation. Downgrading to cells with excess demand is likely to involve fairly high levels of general human capital because the existence of excess demand in a cell implies a lack of substitutability among workers which, in turn, is more likely to be associated with relatively high levels of human capital. This process is perfectly compatible with search theory since workers will tend not to commit themselves quickly to costly programmes to augment human capital and because of the presumed sensitivity to the loss of caste that accompanies downgrading.

The labour market is seen as a set of compartmentalised markets among which negligible mobility exists in the short run. The difficulties of mobility (in the long run) may be asymmetric in that downward mobility is easier than upward mobility (because upward mobility is constrained by the availability of resources and limitations deriving from the birth vita). Given that the acquisition of human capital, particularly human capital in a different industry, becomes more difficult with age, mobility is greater among the young.

When the supply within a cell is governed by a union, it may command a premium and particularly so if the industry itself is highly profitable. The rate of profit or product price influences management's capacity to pay a premium wage. When the market for the end product is imperfectly competitive, management may yield to union demands with the expectation that higher costs can be made up by introducing new, more capital-intensive machinery or by passing the increase on to the ultimate user. Alternatively spontaneous price increases by corporations can indicate the buoyancy of the product market and may stimulate union demands. Whatever the mechanism, the wage premium is the result of imperfections in the product or factor market when, as is usual with industrial unions, there is great substitutability between union members and other workers in the economy. Canterbery refers to this premium as 'the economic profits allocated to workers per hour of effort' (p.22). Under these conditions, the wage rate is determined by the level of production. In the long run, an asymmetry can affect this mechanism too. If the premium is acquired when times are good and there is resistance to its renunciation when conditions in the industry deteriorate, employment will be affected by the wage premium.

The purpose of the vita theory was to develop a theory of income distribution with a primary emphasis on the determination of wage rates. Its use as a vehicle for analysis of the adjustment process is a tribute to the breadth of analytic framework which Canterbery has generated. Most important for the purposes of this book are the recognition of the time dimension in mobility among compartmentalised markets and the identification of the existence and asymmetry of impediments to the free flow of labour among markets.

Appendix B: The Legal Institutional Environment for Protection in the US

There are four main bases on which an industry (enterprises or unions) may formally seek relief from foreign competition in the US. These are injurious import competition when there is no allegation of 'unfair' practice; disruption as a result of imports of an article or commodity from a Communist country; to safeguard national security; and 'unfair trade practices' which comprise dumping, foreign governmental subsidies of exports and infringements of a US patent in imported merchandise. There exists as well a programme of Trade Adjustment Assistance (TAA).

'Injurious import competition, when there is no allegation of unfair practice', is covered by Sections 201–3 of the Trade Act of 1974. These sections authorise the President to provide import relief when an article is being imported into the US in such increased quantities as to be a substantial cause of serious injury. The decision on the legitimacy of any claim for relief is made by the US International Trade Commission which, if it decides affirmatively will recommend certain protective measures to the President. Import relief can take many forms, ranging from straightforward tariffs to tariff-quotas to quotas and even orderly marketing arrangements. Relief may not be given for more than five years in the first instance with the possibility of an extension of relief for a further period of three years after a review by the Commission. There is a discrepancy in the legislation that weakens the force of the Commissions's recommendation: the Commission must make its decision on the narrow issue of injury to the domestic industry; the President *must* take into account such considerations as the national interest and the effects of relief on consumers.

'Market disruption' is legislated under Section 406 of the Trade Act of 1974. The criterion in such a claim is the rate of increase, absolute or relative, of imports of an article such as to be 'a significant cause of material injury, or threat therefore, to such domestic industry'. Under this criterion any action taken by the President, on the advice of the International Trade Commission, must be directed only at the communist country or countries from which the injurious imports come. Presumably the basis for singling out communist countries is that their economic system allows international prices to depart substantially from what would be market-determined costs and it is impossible to identify such sales as sales at 'less than fair value'.

The legislation of the criterion for safeguarding national security is contained in Section 232 of the Trade Expansion Act of 1962. In this instance the arbiter is a cabinet member (usually the Secretary of the Treasury) rather than the US International Trade Commission. Once presidential action has been taken, the President must report to the Congress on the actions taken and on the underlying reasoning.

'Unfair trade practices' essentially involve sales in the US of articles at 'less than fair value'. The source of the subsidised price may be an attempt by commercial enterprises to penetrate a market by selling at a subsidised price or may be a subsidy or grant paid, directly or indirectly, by the exporter's government. Typically, the mechanism for establishing sales at 'less than fair market value' is tortuous. The responsibility for determining whether the good in question has been 'dumped' or subsidised rests with the Secretary of the Treasury, but if dumping or subsidy is established, it is the International Trade Commission which has the responsibility for determining whether the US industry had suffered (or was likely to suffer) material injury. Legislative authority for both kinds of 'unfair practice' were updated in the Trade Agreements Act of 1979.

Under the standard procedures the delay between lodging a complaint alleging foreign dumping, and the instigation of remedial action by the Administration, could be protracted. In response to severe competition for the US steel industry from foreign steel, a new procedure was instituted for complaints of alleged dumping of steel: the trigger-price mechanism (see Walter, 1979, pp. 165–71). The whole purpose of specifying trigger prices would constitute *prima facie* evidence for dumping, and would therefore allow an anti-dumping duty to be paid in escrow at the time of import pending the establishment of dumping. This device has not proved to be a success because of the difficulties involved in computing trigger prices, particularly in a world of flexible rates of exchange in which the most efficient foreign producers (whose costs form the basis for the trigger-price computations) change according to fluctuations in rates of exchange. This mechanism lapsed when the Reagan Administration retaliated against the filing of a formal 'dumping complaint' by US Steel in 1982.

There exists, as well, a measure for countering any subsidy paid directly or indirectly on imported merchandise by foreign governments. These 'countervailing duties' are instituted jointly by the Department of Commerce and International Trade Commission; the Department of Commerce decides whether a subsidy has in fact been applied, and the Commission decides on (actual or potential) damage to a US industry (Trade Agreement Act of 1979).

Where imported merchandise infringes a US patent, the imported merchandise can be excluded under Section 341 of the Trade Act of 1974 (amending Section 337 of the Tariff Act of 1930).

All four mechanisms resulting only in adjustment-retarding measures indicate a lack of concern with the process of adjustment. Presumably no adjustment is needed because all the disturbances are non-sustainable. TAA, in contrast,is explicitly concerned with adjustment. It was inaugurated in the Trade Expansion Act of 1962 under the Kennedy Administration. Its most important provisions were:

(a) to supplement the income of displaced labour in terms more generous than

standard unemployment insurance by increasing the support level and
extending the period of coverage
(b) to encourage displaced labour to make use of existing programmes for
retraining and job placement and to provide relocation grants for displaced
workers moving to take up employment in a new part of the country
(c) to provide injured firms with special tax privileges
(d) to provide free technical consultations and low-interest loan guarantees

These benefits were to be applied to workers and firms for whom US trade
liberalisation was the *major* cause of their injury. In fact, the legislation was
administered so stringently that no adjustment assistance was granted or
approved until the early 1970s, when the eligibility requirements were
interpreted less strictly. The US Trade Act of 1974 liberalised the conditions
for eligibility by making the cause of injury any change in international trading
conditions, and by requiring that imports need contribute 'importantly' to the
injury. Payments to workers (except for the extension for workers engaged in
training), and tax benefits to firms, are designed to ease the burden of
industrial decline rather than to facilitate a reallocation of resources. TAA as a
whole hardly qualifies as 'purposive adjustment', but the provision of
subsidised loans, technical consultation, training, counselling and relocation
grants are all purposive adjustments which facilitate the transfer of resources
to competitive enterprises. (Note that consultation and low-interest loans to
firms are more likely to improve the efficiency of the injured firms than to lead
to a reallocation of resources to another industry in which the US has a
comparative advantage. Once a realistic degree of efficiency has been reached,
then no further benefit can be derived from this type of action, and if the
competitiveness of the domestic industry is declining secularly the net result of
this aspect of TAA is also simply 'adjustment retardation'.)

With the exception of the programme of TAA and the associated
procedures which allow industries to petition for import relief, the role of the
US government in the adjustment process is negligible. As noted above, much
of TAA is adjustment-retarding rather than a positive force in the process of
the reallocation of resources from a declining into an expanding industry.
TAA seeks to slow down the required rate of adjustment by encouraging
contracting industries to reduce costs and to increase their operational
efficiency. Such actions merely delay the inevitable if the relieved industry
suffers from an insuperable cost disadvantage. Similarly, payments to workers
reduce the hardship involved in displacement by imports and can also retard
the process of seeking employment in another internationally competitive
industry.

In keeping with its avowed economic philosophy, the Reagan
Administration is prepared to leave the process of adjustment to market
forces. Attempts to phase out the TAA programme in the fiscal years 1982
budget were unsuccessful although the amount budgeted was relatively small
(£250 million). Since Worker Adjustment Assistance, once granted, is a right
and not subject to further screening or review, this allocation may prove to be
unduly optimistic. (One detailed estimate put the amount required at between
£750 million and £1000 million (see Miller and Van Erden, 1981).) In contrast,
assistance to enterprises does require prolonged screening, and there is no

automaticity of benefits but it would be difficult to bias the outcome of eligibility hearings for budget reasons.

As noted above, the TAA programme allows for assistance to be given to trade-impacted firms, workers and communities. The programme to aid communities has never been invoked because the Economic Development and Adjustment Assistance Plan serves the same purpose, and has much less stringent conditions. The TAA programme for firms requires that the firm be certified as having been 'importantly' injured by foreign competition, and it can then apply for financial and/or technical assistance. Technical assistance consists of the provision of management and marketing consultancy services at the expense of the Federal Government. Financial assistance provides loans or loan guarantee limits of $1 to $3 million. The size of the financial assistance available effectively limits the programme to 'small business'. From April 1975 until the fiscal year ending 30 September 1980, 972 firms had been certified as eligible for TAA, and assistance was given in the amount of approximately $328 million. More than 80 per cent of these funds were used for financial assistance. The pace of certification was increasing as almost 100 firms were certified during the last quarter of (calendar year) 1980, compared with 90 firms in the whole of calendar year 1979. This increase in applications is likely to have resulted jointly from greater awareness of the programme and greater pressures from imports on small business. The programme, except insofar as it improves a firm's efficiency and reestablishes an enterprise as potentially competitive with imports, is merely adjustment retarding. It plays little role, if any, in reallocating resources out of industries in which the US has a competitive disadvantage.

The payments of benefits to workers follow similar procedures, and with the exception of payments made to workers for retraining and relocation, are adjustment retarding in the sense that the workers are more likely to hope for recall to their old employer. Once the workers have been certified as eligible for TAA benefits assistance, they are assured of compensation which exceeds that available to workers laid off for 'domestic reasons' in both duration and amount.

There is also a programme of TAA for injured communities (which rely heavily upon injured industries). No payments have ever been made under this programme. The community programme is currently scheduled to expire in 1982, and the firm and worker assistance programmes in 1983. These programmes have been extended by one year virtually without change in the procedures and eligibility requirements.

The MFA sets a pattern for bilateral arrangements between developed importers of textiles and apparel and developing exporters, the general principle recognises that unrestrained imports of textiles and apparel would cause damaging reallocation problems in many developed countries, and imports into those countries must therefore be restrained. The important exporters are limited in the quantity of their exports by bilateral agreements which are generally supposed to allow for positive rates of growth or imports. The restrictive measure is a quota which is set for different types of commodities (yarns, cloth and apparel of different kinds). The bilaterals cover apparel made out of cotton, wool and/or man-made fibres. One American union representative has alleged that the US is relatively generous in the establishment of quotas in its bilateral agreements. In the event that no agreement can be reached between an exporter and the importing nation, the importer reserves the right to impose quotas unilaterally. The US has recently imposed quotas on imports from the People's Republic of China in this way.

TAA traces its rationale (*raison d'être*) to three arguments, two economic and one political. The economic argument deals with equity and efficiency. Equity provides assistance to workers laid off because of international events and really requires some proof that workers disemployed as a result of international events have greater difficulty in finding alternative employment (or suffer a larger reduction in income) than workers laid off because of changes in the domestic economy. In fact, there appears to be no substantial difference between the two groups (Aho and Bayard, 1984): 'The TAA population does not appear to be very different from the control group (domestic displacements covered by unemployment insurance) in terms of either occupation and demographic characteristics or in terms of adjustment costs'.

The efficiency argument is based on the proposition that large-scale layoffs in trade-impacted industries will result in longer periods of unemployment (than that due to domestic causes) because of congestion in the appropriate labour markets. The argument has three dimensions: trade-impacted industries are likely to be the major employers in particular regions of the country, widespread layoffs in those industries will cause the local labour markets to become congested, and laid-off workers will find greater than average difficulty in finding employment in another industry. When laid-off workers all have quite similar skills, an excess supply (congestion) in the labour market for that skill level would exist. The probability of being able to find employment in another industry would be *pro tanto* less and adjustment would be impeded.

The third argument for TAA is one of political efficiency, in that it would not have been possible in 1962 or 1974 to ensure the passage of trade liberalisation authority without some promised payment to anyone hurt by trade liberalisation (Aho and Bayard, 1984): 'The political argument (for government intervention in the adjustment process) is that certain interest groups have sufficient political power to block or delay socially beneficial changes unless they are generously compensated and otherwise assisted'.

Certainly the introduction of Worker Adjustment Assistance in the two acts was important in reducing the effectiveness of the opposition of the Labour Movement to multilateral tariff negotiations, as well as in reducing pressures within organised labour to present stronger arguments. In addition to the direct effects on lobbying by pressure groups, the existence of a TAA programme is also likely to reduce public sympathy for protectionist positions.

The direction of TAA and import-relief programmes in the US is largely adjustment-retarding. In an attempt to improve the adjustment-promoting effects of TAA, the Comptroller General of the United States has argued that income-maintenance benefits paid to workers should be tied to retraining and/or relocation (Comptroller General of the United States, 1980). But the US does not have an effective record of achievement in retraining workers in peacetime.

The US Federal Government has several programmes in 'worker education, training, placement and mobility', but the federal role is not a highly significant one. One reason for this is that a great part of total federal expenditure in this area is disbursed to the individual states in the form of block grants. Equally, tradition in the US leaves the task of matching vacancies and employment seekers to the marketplace. Many of the programmes in force are tailored quite closely and specifically to individual programmes or identifiable groups such as the handicapped, disadvantaged youth or veterans. The net result of all of this effort and expenditure is that the federal government is not an important force in enhancing the mobility of disemployed workers.

Many of the programmes are not suitable for the retraining of persons with substantial work experience, and are designed primarily for new entrants to the labour force.

The TAA programme of Worker Adjustment Assistance allows an extra 26 weeks of benefits for those in training, but only a few availed themselves of federal assistance between 1975 and 1979. During this period, nearly half a million workers received compensation under the TAA programme, but only 17 500 took advantage of training funds, 2500 of the job search allowances and 1700 of relocation allowances. The other major programme is the Comprehensive Employment and Training Act (CETA), but most of these funds are devoted to training persons who are unskilled and have limited educational backgrounds. Title II of CETA provides authority for a full range of manpower services, including training, work experience and upgrading and retraining. Eligibility for these programmes is restricted to the economically disadvantaged and unemployed, except for 'upgrading and retraining' provided to those already in the labour force. This segment of the programme is limited to 6.4 per cent of federal funds received. There exist also so-called 'private sector' programmes whereby firms which hire persons from one of the identifiable groups receive tax credits of up to $4500 spread over two years.

The Reagan Administration's avowed intent to expose industries to the chill winds of competition, both domestically and from foreign sources, has been endorsed in the international trade arena by Ambassador Bill Brock, special trade representative of the President:

> We don't believe Japanese imports have created the problem (for the U.S. Automobile Industry) and we don't believe the elimination of imports would solve the problem . . . It is now up to our industry to retool, increase its productivity, increase the quality of its product and produce in a competitive fashion . . . This administration believes companies have the right to fail. (*Forbes*, 8 June 1981, p. 160)

The commitment is less than complete. Brock endorsed the extension of MFA upon its expiration at the end of 1981 in Brussels on 21 May 1981. He recognised that this position was something of a second-best solution. Of course, political reality intrudes here: two of the administration's staunchest allies in the US Senate came from North Carolina where reliance upon textiles and apparel is the highest in the country.

Prior to its demise, the Carter administration had proposed two new measures which were likely to have proved positive contributions to the adjustment problem:

(a) a proposed tax credit to offset the increase in the employers' and employee's share of the social security tax (in this way helping the more labour-intensive and low-skill industries more likely to be subject to pressure from imports).

(b) proposed additional federal investment of $600 million over two years for a combination programme on incentives to retrain or relocate workers into growth sectors and expanded funding of the 'upgrading and retraining' portion of the CETA programme.

Probably retraining and upgrading would be most effectively accomplished by on-the-job training, but under current American programmes workers lose benefits if they accept this type of retraining.

Notes and References

1 THE PRESENT NEED TO RECONSIDER THE FREE-TRADE DOCTRINE

1. Marshall (1920, pp. 378–80) does recognise that the training up of human capital is likely to take longer than the addition of a piece of capital equipment, and defines the long run as the new equilibrium when both skilled worker and machine are available. Common usage is to consider the long run as the period required to add tangible capital, and the reference in the text adopts this practice.
2. Even if it were to hold eventually, the social costs would be too great to permit inactivity. The problem here is analogous to that of the thirties: no one has proven or can prove that the economy would stay depressed forever.
3. On this subject, see the very detailed and insightful paper by Messerlein (1981).

3 'DOMESTIC INEFFICIENCY' AND CONDITIONAL PROTECTION

1. As will be shown in the next chapter, the concept of conditional protection can also be applied to applications of phase-out protection.
2. Note that the wage premium will not be achieved if the industry is constrained by import competition.
3. Always assuming the X-inefficiency at Ford is not equalled in all other activities: see an anticipation of this point in 'industry modifiers' in Gray (1976a, pp. 40–3).
4. Note that, for international trade purposes, the concept of X-efficiency must be transformed to an industry instead of a firm attribute. All the other causes of domestic inefficiency are, by definition, industry–wide.
5. In April 1982 the Reagan Administration announced the imposition of a tariff increase of tenfold, and will raise the price of imported large motorcycles in the US by more than 10 per cent. The Japanese price before the protective action was about $1500 to $2000 less than that of American-made motorcycles of this kind. The increase in protection is, ostensibly, temporary.
6. It is important to distinguish between lack of managerial effort (which is one aspect of X-inefficiency) and managerial mistakes, which can be coupled with

maximum effort. These are not an example of X-*in*efficiency, they are plain and simple errors. Compare analysis of the US television industry's failure to combat Japanese competition in that industry (Tsurumi and Tsurumi, 1980).

7. Clearly the speed with which the cooperation between labour and management will be achieved depends upon the climate of antagonism between them. Cooperation will come much more slowly in the US than in Japan. The strength of the argument for a hands-off policy is, therefore, related to the country's culture.

4   THE PROBLEM OF THE *RATE* OF ADJUSTMENT

1. Cf. Chapter 3.
2. For simplicity of exposition, this section continues to assume that the disturbance causes no change in total jobs.
3. The implicit assumption is that the disturbance has created a surplus of low-skilled workers and a shortage of workers with high skill levels.
4. The broad version implies an aggregate demand argument for protection. Because of the likelihood of retaliation by trading partners, and because of the existence of more effective instrument variables, a deficiency of aggregate demand is not an adequate argument for protection: gains from trade will be lost without any compensating increase in national employment.
5. The degree of aggregation in a two-digit data base also robs Krueger's study (1980) of any significant import. As Finger (1975) has shown, factor mixes vary within industries at this level of aggregation as much or more than they do between industries.
6. The suitability of the measure used to the abstract (theoretical) concept is crucial to the accuracy of empirical work, and is referred to by Margenau (1966) as the quality of the 'rules of correspondence'.
7. While the text presents the argument in terms of an individual worker, the total cost is the summation of all lost income by all displaced workers. The physical capital might find a productive use in the country which now has the comparative advantage, especially if a multinational corporation is involved in the reallocation of production (Kojima, 1973). This would be reflected in the salvage value.
8. The cost of protection includes any loss in total consumer welfare (as noted above). If the protection is given in the form of a subsidy, then the real cost of the subsidy should also be included.
9. There is always a stronger case to be made for positive manpower policies than for protection if positive policies can resolve the problem, because such policies improve the capability of the economy to adjust in the future to disturbances that may have their origin in either the foreign or the domestic sector.

5   THE POSSIBILITY OF PERMANENT UNEMPLOYMENT

1. Leontief (1982) addresses this problem.
2. Unemployment in this context must be defined in terms of the money wage needed

in the rich nations for the welfare subsistence level of income.
3. The wide range of substitutability shown in Figure 5.1 is not untoward if the composite commodity includes a large number of individual goods with widely varying capital/labour intensities.
4. The notion of composite goods is developed fully in Samuelson (1947). It achieves its analytic usefulness at the fairly substantial cost of assuming away all changes in the mix of goods making up the composite.
5. Hager (1982) is not optimistic on this score: 'The implicit assumption by adjustment optimists that there is equilibrium in a free exchange between high-cost and low-cost areas of production which maintains something like full employment in the high-cost area is implausible to the point of being disingenuous'.
6. Between 1975 and 1979, nearly half a million American workers received compensation under the Trade Adjustment Assistance Act but only 17 500 took advantage of funds made available to those who underwent training to enhance their skills.
7. Krueger (1974) develops the argument of the rent-seeking pressure group. It may be worth noting that there is likely to be an asymmetry. Pressure groups will try harder to maintain the standard of living which they have once enjoyed; if that implies acquiring a quasi-rent under the new conditions, then they will try to achieve a previously unattained quasi-rent.
8. This merely transfers some of the burdens to the frustrated exporters on the grounds, presumably, that they will have had greater practice at bearing them: see Chapter 7 below.

6 IMPASSE IN NORTH–SOUTH POLICY FORMULATION

1. A larger scale (Utopian) proposal is developed in Chapter 7.
2. Note that both McFadzean (1981) and Curzon *et al.* (1981) are products of the Trade Policy Research Centre. But for the fact that the Centre is a highly respected (and highly respectable) institution, the kinship of the two reports might be seen as weakening the argument of this section. The decision to focus on these two reports derives in part from their authoritative authorship, and in part from their clarity. The McFadzean Report, in particular, merits consideration by all those involved in issues relating to the international aspects of economic development.
3. The Brandt Commission is the usual title given to the Independent Commission on International Development Issues (1980).
4. The terms 'clothing' and 'apparel' may be used interchangeably. 'Clothing' is the preferred description in Europe and 'apparel' in the US.
5. For a full description of MFA see Keesing and Wolf (1980).
6. MFA was renewed in December 1981, much along the lines of the original version. The gloomy forecast of the Report of fixed market shares was not incorporated.
7. See Section III below in this chapter.
8. See Appendix B for a description of the very structured system which prevails in the US.
9. Gray (1982) tests the effect of imports from Africa for the UK and West Germany: the proportionate increases in the ratio remain effectively constant.

10. Fieleke (1981) shows the pattern of industrial employment in manufacturing underwent more severe changes in between 1973 and 1977 in the US than either Japan or the UK.

7 SOUTHERN DEMANDS AND A CONSTRUCTIVE ALTERNATIVE

1. The North is always available in southern countries to serve as a scapegoat to be blamed for non-performance. The proposals could be seen simply in this light but that would amount to an excessive interpretation of reality.
2. The origin of this idea was the Development Advisory Committee of the OECD.
3. The 'consensus statement' of UNCTAD VI contained a reaffirmation of this goal but the US disassociated itself from the statement and many other developed nations indicated that their acceptance of the statement was subject to some reservations or qualifications (UNCTAD, 1983, p. 2).
4. In the 'consensus statement' of UNCTAD VI, the developed nations 'committed themselves to halt protectionism by fully implementing and strictly adhering to standstill provisions'. They also agreed to work systematically towards reducing and eliminating quantitative restrictions and measures (UNCTAD, 1983, p. 4).
5. If lower tariffs resulted in offsetting or partially offsetting non-tariff barriers being imposed, then southern nations would be worse off since GSP does not provide for preferential treatment in non-tariff barriers.
6. Of course, displaced workers exerting political pressures for protection are a straightforward expression of 'selfish interests' but these are sectoral rather than national which seems to be the thrust of Li Ke's remarks.
7. It may be advisable to exclude Greece and, potentially Spain and Portugal from this criterion.

8 FREE TRADE AMONG THE INDUSTRIALISED NATIONS?

1. This list is not intended to be definitive, and there exist other obvious candidates for inclusion.
2. What is being considered here is technically a free trade area in all manufactured goods: zero impediments to internal trade in manufactures and individual nationally-determined impediments to outsiders.
3. Several US computer firms are manufacturing in France, either through joint ventures or wholly-owned subsidiaries. Given the cost disadvantages of France within the Common Market, it can be presumed that these firms saw a French manufacturing presence as offering leverage in supplying the government sector.
4. Dionne refers to this event as the 'second "Battle of Poitiers" '. Charles Martel stopped the Moorish army at Poitiers in 732 AD. It would be more correct to refer to the modern event as the second French victory at Poitiers since France suffered a humbling defeat at Poitiers in 1356.

9 SUMMARY AND CONCLUSIONS

1. If only *pour encourager les autres.*

2. Michalski (1983) identifies the post-adjustment target in terms of the ability of the economy to absorb minor shocks without instigating unemployment or inflationary pressures by virtue of an acceptable rate of economic growth and the absence of suppressed maladjustments. Michalski can be interpreted as arguing that the first task of adjustment policy is to adapt the economy to fit the new circumstances and to have the set of factor costs adapt as well. If income-distributional problems need to be incorporated in the new state, they should be solved by transfer rather than by supporting markets for end products at unrealistic prices.

3. Kempe (1984) suggests that the East German Government may understand the process of adjustment in capitalist economies since they chose a period of substantial unemployment in West Germany to allow a large number of refugees to leave Germany, possibly in the simple hope of embarrassing the West Germans.

Bibliography

Aho, C. Michael and T. O. Bayard (1980) 'American Trade Adjustment Assistance after Five Years', *The World Economy*, 3 November, 359–760.

Aho, C. Michael and T. O. Bayard. (1984) 'Costs and Benefits of Trade Adjustment Assistance' in R. E. Baldwin and A. O. Krueger (eds), *Structure and Evolution of Recent US Trade Policy* (University of Chicago Press).

Aho, C. Michael and James Orr (1981) 'Trade-sensitive Employment: Who are the Affected Workers?', *Monthly Labor Review*, February.

Akamatsu, K. (1962) 'A Historical Pattern of Economic Growth in Developing Countries', *The Developing Economies*, March–August.

Alting von Geusau, Frans A. M. (1977) *The Lomé Conventions and a New International Economic Order* (Leyden: Sinthof).

Barde, Jean-Phillippe (1976) 'National and International Policy Alternatives for Environmental Control and their Economic Implications' In Ingo Walter (ed.), *Studies in International Environmental Economics* (New York: Wiley Interscience), ch. 6.

Bhagwati, Jagdish N. (1977) 'Market Disruption, Export Market Disruption, Compensation and GATT Reform', in Bhagwati (ed.), *The New International Economic Order: The North–South Debate* (Cambridge, Mass.: MIT Press, 1977) 159–79.

Bhagwati, J. and V. K. Ramaswami (1963) 'Domestic Distortion, Tariffs and the Theory of the Optimum Subsidy' *Journal of Political Economy*, 71, 44–50.

Blackhurst, Richard (1981) 'The Twilight of Domestic Economic Policies', *The World Economy*, 4 December.

Borders, William (1981) 'British Steel: Moment of Truth', *New York Times*, 16 January.

Branson, W. A. (1975) 'Global Monetarism and the Monetary Approach to the Balance of Payments: Comment', *Brookings Papers on Economic Activity*, 536–40.

Brenner, Harvey (1976) *Estimating the Social Cost of National Economic Policy: Implications for Mental and Physical Health, and Criminal Aggression* (Washington, DC: Joint Economic Committee, US Congress).

Buss, Dale D. (1983) 'Many Auto Workers Bitterly Blame UAW for Recent Givebacks', *Wall Street Journal*, 13 May.

Cain, Glen (1976) 'The Challenge of Segmented Labor Market Theories to Orthodox Theory: A Survey, *Journal of Economic Literature*, 14, December, 1939–41.

Canterbery, E. Ray (1979) 'A Vita Theory of Personal Income Distribution', *Southern Economic Journal*, 46, July, 12–48.

Canterbery, E. Ray (1980) 'Welfare Economics and the Vita Theory', *Eastern Economic Journal*, VI, January, 1–20.

Carley, W. M. (1980) 'Closing of a Ford Plant Reflects Rising Worry of Car Makers: Quality', *Wall Street Journal*, 16 June.

Caves, Richard E. (1960) *Trade and Economic Structure* (Cambridge, Mass.: Harvard University Press.

Clausen, A. W. (1983) 'Business, The Developing Countries, and the World Bank' (Washington,DC: World Bank, 11 April) (mimeo).

Comptroller General of the United States (1980) *Restricting Trade Act Benefits to Import-affected Who Cannot Find a Job Can Save Millions, Report to the Congress* (Washington, DC: US Government Printing Office).

Corden, W. M. (1971) *The Theory of Protection* (Oxford: Clarendon Press).

Corden, W. M. (1974) *Trade Policy and Economic Welfare* (Oxford: Clarendon Press).

Crandall, R. W. (1981) *The US Steel Industry in Recurring Crisis: Policy Options in a Competitive World* (Washington, DC: The Brookings Institution).

Curzon, G., J. de la Torre, J. B. Donges, A. I. Macbean, J. Waelbroeck and M. Wolf (1981) 'MFA Forever? Future of the Arrangement for Trade in Textiles', *International Issues No. 5* (London: Trade Policy Research Centre).

Curzon Price, Victoria (1980) 'Alternatives to Delayed Structural Adjustment in "Workshop Europe" ', *The World Economy*, 3, September 205–16.

Curzon Price, Victoria (1981) *Industrial Policies in the European Community* (London: Macmillan).

Davidson, Paul (1972) *Money and the Real World* (London: Macmillan).

Deardorff, Alan V. and Robert M. Stern (1983) 'Current Issues in Trade Policy: An Overview', *University of Michigan Institute of Public Policy Studies Discussion Paper No. 185*.

Dionne, E.J. Jr (1983) 'French Lifting Curb on Japanese Video Recorders', *New York Times*, 29 April.

Ferguson, C. E. (1969) *Microeconomic Theory* (rev. edn, Holmwood, Ill.: Irwin).

Fieleke, Norman S. (1981) 'Productivity and Labor Mobility in Japan, the United Kingdom, and the United States', *New England Economic Review*, November–December, 27–36.

Finger, J. M. (1975) 'Trade Overlap and Intra-industry Trade', *Economic Inquiry*, 13, 581–9.

Friedman, Milton (1958) 'Foreign Economic Aid: Means and Objectives', *Yale Review*, 47, Summer, 500–16.

Gray, H. Peter (1972) *The Economics of Business Investment Abroad* (London: Macmillan).

Gray, H. Peter (1973) 'Senile Industry Protection: A Proposal', *Southern Economic Journal*, 39, April, 569–74.

Gray, H. Peter (1976a) *A Generalized Theory of International Trade* (London: Macmillan).

Gray, H. Peter (1976b) Commercial Policy Implications of Environmental Controls', in Ingo Walter (ed.), *Studies in International Environmental*

Economics (New York: Wiley Interscience), ch. 7.

Gray, H. Peter (1979) *International Trade, Investment and Payments* (Boston, Mass.: Houghton Mifflin).

Gray, H. Peter (1982) 'Adjustment Burdens, Potential Protectionism and the Vulnerability of Export-led Growth', *Journal of Economic Development*, 7, July, 7–20.

Gray, H. Peter (1983) 'X-efficiency Theory and International Trade Theory' (mimeo).

Gray, H. Peter (1984) 'The Theory of Adjustment Policy' (mimeo).

Gray, H. Peter and Ingo Walter (1983) 'Investment-related Trade Distortions in Petrochemicals', *Journal of World Trade Law*, 17, July–August, 283–307.

Gray, Jean M. and H. Peter Gray (1982) 'The Multinational Bank: A Financial MNC?', *Journal of Banking and Finance*, 5 March, pp. 33–63.

Hager, Wolfgang (1982) 'North–South Trade and Socio–Economic Autonomy: A Peace Formula', *Trade and Development Unctad Review*, Winter.

Hillman, Arye L. (1977) 'The Case for Terminal Protection for Declining Industries', *Southern Economic Journal*, 44, July, 155–160.

Hillman, Arye L. (1982) 'Declining Industries and Political-support Protectionist Motives', *American Economic Review*, 72, December, 1180–7.

Hindley, Brian and Eri Nicolaides (1983) 'Taking the New Protectionism Seriously', *Thames Essay No. 34*, (London: Trade Policy Research Centre).

Japanese Institute of Labour (1979) 'Labour Unions and Labour-Management Relations', *Japanese Industrial Relations Series, no. 2*.

Johnson, George E. (1978) 'Structural Unemployment Consequences of Job Creation Policies' In John L. Palmer (ed.), *Creating Jobs* (Washington, DC: The Brookings Institution).

Kaldor, N. (1971) 'Conflicts in National Economic Objectives', *Economic Journal*, LXXXI, March, 1–16.

Keesing, D. B. and M. Wolf (1980) 'Textile Quotas Against Developing Countries', *Thames Essay No. 23* (London: Trade Policy Research Centre).

Kempe, Frederick (1984) 'Breaching a Barrier', *Wall Street Journal*, 4 May.

Keynes, J. M. (1936) *The General Theory of Employment, Interest and Money*. (London: Macmillan).

Kojima, Kiyoshi (1973) 'A Macroeconomic Approach to Foreign Direct Investment', *Hitotsubashi Journal of Economics*, 14, June.

Krauss, Melvyn B. (1978) *The New Protectionism: The Welfare State and International Trade* (New York University Press).

Kreinin, M. I. and J. M. Finger (1976) 'A Critical Survey of the New International Economic Order', *Journal of World Trade Law*, 10, November–December.

Krueger, A. O. (1974) 'The Political Economy of the Rent-seeking Society', *American Economic Review*, 64, May, 291–303.

Krueger, A. O. (1980) 'LDC Manufacturing Production and Implications for OECD Comparative Advantage', in Irving Leveson and Jimmy W. Wheeler (eds), *Western Economies in Transition* (Boulder, Col.: Westview Press), pp. 219–50.

Leamer, Edward E. (1980) 'Welfare Computations and the Optimal Staging of Tariff Reductions in Models with Adjustment Costs', *Journal of International Economics*, 10, 21–34.

Leibenstein, Harvey (1978) 'On the Basic Proposition of X-efficiency Theory' *American Economic Review*, 68, May, 328–32.

Leibenstein, Harvey (1979) 'X-efficiency: From Concept to Theory', *Challenge*, September–October, 13–22.

Leontief, Wassily W. (1982) 'The Distribution of Work and Income', *Scientific American*, 247, No. 3, 188–204.

Lorenz, Detlef (1982) 'Notes on Unequal Exchange between Developing and Industrialized Nations', *Intereconomics*, January–February, 13–19.

Lorenz, Detlef (1983) 'Industrial Imports from the Asian NICs, Principal Adjustment Problems and European Strategies of Protectionism', in *Patterns of Growth and Structural Change* (Hawaii).

Love, Howard M. (1981) 'Statement', *Steel '81* (Washington, DC: American Iron and Steel Institute).

Magee, Stephen P. (1977) 'Multinational Corporations, the Industry Technology Cycle and Development', *Journal of World Trade Law*, 11, July–August, 297–321.

Malmgren, Harald B. (1983) 'Threats to the Multilateral System', in William R. Cline (ed.), *Trade Policy in the 1980s*, (Washington, DC: Institute of International Economics), 189–201.

Margenau, Henry (1966) 'What is a Theory?', in Sherman Roy Krupp (ed.), *The Structure of Economic Science*, (Englewood Cliffs, N.J. Prentice-Hall) 25–38.

Marshall, Alfred (1920) *Principles of Economics* 8th edn (London: Macmillan).

Marshall, Ray (1983) 'Health and Unemployment', presented at 111th American Public Health Association Annual Meeting, Dallas, Texas, 15 November.

McFadzean, Lord, of Kelvinside *et al.* (1981) 'Global Strategy for Growth', *Special Report No. 1* (London: Trade Policy Research Centre).

McKersie, R. B. and Werner Sengenberger (1983) *Job Losses in Major Industries* (Paris: OECD).

McKinnon, R. I. (1964) 'Foreign Exchange Constraints on Economic Development and Efficient Aid Allocation', *Economic Journal*, LXXXIV, June, 388–409.

Meade, J. E. (1952) *A Geometry of the Theory of International Trade* (London: George Allen & Unwin).

Meade, J. E. (1955) *Trade and Welfare* (Oxford University Press).

Meade, J. E. (1956) *Trade and Welfare: Mathematical Supplement* (Oxford University Press).

Meade, James (1983) 'A New Keynesian Approach to Full Employment', *Lloyds Bank Review*, October, 1–18.

Messerlein, P. A. (1981) 'The Political Economy of Protectionism: The Bureaucratic Case', *Weltwirtschaftliches Archiv*, 117, 469–96.

Michalski, Wolfgang (1983) 'The Need for Positive Adjustment Policies in the 1980's', *Intereconomics*, January–February, 42–8.

Mill, John Stuart (1909) *Principles of Political Economy* (London:

Longmans).

Miller, M. J. and J. D. Van Erden (1981) 'The Increase in Trade Adjustment Assistance Benefits – Program and Policy Implications of the Auto Recession', paper presented at the Annual Meeting of the Western Economic Association, San Francisco, 5 July.

Murray, Tracy (1977) *Generalized System of Preferences* (London: Macmillan).

Myrdal, Gunnar (1957) *Rich Lands and Poor* (New York: Harper & Row; English Title: *Economic Theory and Underdeveloped Regions*).

Nordheimer, Jon (1983) 'Europe's Joblessness Begets Generation of Despair', *New York Times*, 17 April, 16.

OECD (1972) *Recommendation of the Council on Guiding Principles Concerning International Economic Aspects of Environmental Policies* (Paris: OECD, 6 June).

OECD (1979) *The Impact of the Newly Industrializing Countries* (Paris: OECD).

Ohlin, B. Per-Ove Hesselborn, and Per Magnus Wijkman (eds) (1977) *The International Allocation of Economic Activity* (London: Macmillan).

Parsons, D. O. (1980) 'Unemployment, the Allocation of Labor, and Optimal Government Intervention', *American Economic Review*, 70, December, 626–35.

Patel, I. G. (1974) 'A New International Economic Order?', *Indian Economic Review*, April, 3.

Rattner, Steven (1981) 'A Tale of Two Ford Plants', *New York Times*, 13 October.

Reder, Melvin W. (1982) 'Chicago Economics: Permanence and Change', *The Journal of Economic Literature*, 20, March, 1–38.

Ricardo, David (1911) *The Principles of Political Economy and Taxation* (London: Dent).

Roffe, P. (1977) 'International Code of Conduct on Transfer of Technology', *Journal of World Trade Law*, March–April, 186–191.

Rom, Michael (1979) *The Role of Tariff Quotas in Commercial Policy* (London: Macmillan).

Samuelson, P. A. (1939) 'The Gains from International Trade', *Canadian Journal of Economics and Political Science*, V, May, 195–205.

Samuelson, Paul A. (1947) *Foundations of Economic Analysis* (Cambridge, Mass.: Harvard University Press).

Schultze, Charles L. (1983) 'Industrial Policy: A Solution in Search of a Problem', *California Management Review*, 25, Summer, 5–15.

Scitovsky, Tibor (1950) 'A Reconsideration of the Theory of Tariffs', in Howard S. Ellis and Lloyd A. Metzler, *Readings in the Theory of International Trade* (Philadelphia: AEA and the Blakiston Company), 358–89.

Servan-Schreiber, Jean-Jacques (1969) *The American Challenge* (New York: Avon).

Smith, Adam (1976) *The Wealth of Nations* (University of Chicago Press).

Terkel, Studs (1979) 'The Shirt Off Your Back', transcript of a television show produced by WGBH, Boston, Mass.

Tinbergen, J. (1970) *On the Theory of Economic Policy* (Amsterdam: North

Holland).

Törnqvist, Gunnar (1977) 'The Location of Economic Activity: A City-systems Perspective: Comment', in Ohlin *et al.* (eds) *The International Allocation of Economic Activity* (London: Macmillan).

Tsanacas, Demetri (1982) 'The Impact of the Lomé Convention and the Generalized System of Preferences', unpublished PhD dissertation, Rutgers University, New Brunswick, New Jersey.

Tsurumi, H. and Y. Tsurumi (1980) 'A Bayesian Test of the Product Life-Cycle Hypothesis as Applied to the US Demand for Color-TV Sets', *International Economic Review*, 21, October, 583–97.

Tsurumi, H. and Y. Tsurumi (1984) 'Product Life-cycles and Japanese Multinationals in the United States', in Manoranjan Dutta (ed.), *Studies in United States–Asia Economic Relations* (Durham, NC: Acorn).

UNCTAD (1983) *Bulletin*, June, July, August.

Usher, Dan (1963a) 'The Transportation Bias in Comparisons of National Income', *Economica*, 30, 140–58.

Usher, Dan (1963b) 'The Thai National Income at United Kingdom Prices', *Bulletin of the Oxford Institute of Economics and Statistics*, 25 August, 199–214.

Walter, Ingo (1979) 'Protection of Industries in Trouble – the Case of Iron and Steel', *The World Economy*, 8 155–87.

Walter, Ingo (1981–2) 'Crisis in Trade Policy', *NYU business*, Fall–Winter, 16–20.

Walter, Ingo (1983) 'Structural Adjustment and Trade Policy in the International Steel Industry', in Williams R. Cline (ed.), *Trade Policy in the 1980s* (Washington, DC: Institute for International Economics), 483–525.

Wood, Geoffrey E. (1975) 'Senile Industry Protection: Comment', *Southern Economic Journal*, 41, January, 535–7.

Index